CAPITAL STRUCTURE AND FIRM PERFORMANCE

CAPITAL STRUCTURE AND FIRM PERFORMANCE

ARVIN GHOSH

With the collaboration of
Francis Cai
Richard H. Fosberg

Transaction Publishers
New Brunswick (U.S.A.) and London (U.K.)

First paperback edition 2012

This book is printed on acid-free paper that meets the American National Standard for Permanence of Paper for Printed Library Materials.

Library of Congress Catalog Number: 2007030919
ISBN: 978-1-4128-0710-4 (cloth); 978-1-4128-4755-1 (paper)
Printed in the United States of America

Library of Congress Cataloging-in-Publication Data

Ghosh, Arvin, 1937-

Capital structure and firm performance / Arvin Ghosh, with the collaboration of Francis Cai and Richard H. Fosberg.

p. cm.

Includes bibliographical references and index.

ISBN 978-1-4128-0710-4 (alk. paper)

1. Corporations--Finance--Mathematical models. 2. Capital--Mathematical models. 3. Organizational effectiveness. I. Cai, Francis. II. Fosberg, Richard H. III. Title.

HG4012.G54 2007
332'.041--dc22

2007030919

To

Jane Cai

Fei Fosberg

&

In the loving memory
of
Kay Ghosh

Contents

Preface

Capital Structure Theory is one of the most important areas of finance. As Modigliani and Miller opened up the field with their seminal article in 1958, the paper generated many controversies that resulted from comparing their theory to the real world situations. Two competing theories have emerged over the years—the optimal capital structure theory and the pecking order theory. While hundreds of articles have been written on the subject, this is the first time that a book has been written tying together firm performance and underlying capital structure. We hope that our attempt to do so is not in vain and that we have opened new grounds to carry on the research further.

In this research monograph, we have examined the relationship between the financial performance of firms and their capital structures. Chapter 1 is an overview of the controversies regarding capital structure theories. In chapter 2, we have tested statistically both the optimal capital structure and pecking order theories. In chapter 3, we have used the binomial approach to test the capital structure theories. Chapter 4 analyzes the determinants of capital structure, while chapter 5 discusses the role of market power in determining capital structure decisions. In chapter 6, we have probed into new stock offerings and stockholders' returns, and in chapter 7, we have analyzed capital structure and executive compensation. Chapter 8 looks into debt financing and ownership structure, while chapters 9 and 10 discuss the relationship between capital structure and firm profitability—a hotbed of controversy in the capital structure realm.

Chapter 11 summarizes the principal findings presented in the previous chapters. Here we also discuss the latest development in the field of capital structure. While we do not claim this to be the last word on the subject, we hope the debate about capital structure will continue as we attempt to understand its influence on the financial performance of firms more fully.

1

Introduction
Capital Structure Theory: An Overview

Modern capital structure theory began with the path-breaking article of Professors Modigliani and Miller in 1958. Before that we had some vague ideas about the effects of debt and equity issues on capital structure, but no systematic and analytical framework on the subject. Shortly after the Modigliani-Miller article, David Durant had published the costs of debt and equity funds for business in Ezra Solomon's *The Management of Corporate Capital* (ed., 1959). There he introduced two approaches: the Net Income approach and the Net Operating Income approach. In the Net Income approach he showed that a firm can lower its cost of capital and increase its valuation continually with the use of debt funds. But his critical assumption that debt does not become increasingly risky in the minds of investors and creditors as the degree of leverage is increased is a rather unrealistic assumption, to say the least.

Similarly, in his Net Operating Income approach, Durant has assumed that the overall capitalization rate of the firm is constant for all degrees of leverage—an increase in the use of supposedly "cheaper" debt is exactly offset by the increase in the equity-capitalization rate. Thus the weighted average cost of capital composed of debt and equity remain unchanged for all degrees of leverage. According to the Net Operating Income approach, the real cost of debt and the real cost of equity are the same, and there is no optimal capital structure.

Durant's approaches to capital structure theory had been purely definitional and had no behavioral significance. That was provided by Modigliani and Miller's 1958 article which gave a rigorous proof of the independence of firm valuation and the cost of capital in a firm's capital structure.

Modigliani-Miller Theorems

In their seminal article, Modigliani and Miller (henceforth MM) proposed that changes in capital structure has no long-term effect on the value of the firm and that the value of the firm is independent of its bond/stock financing mix. MM built their model on the following main assumptions: (1) the capital market is perfect; (2) there are no taxes; (3) there are no bankruptcy and transaction costs; (4) investors can borrow at the same rate as corporations, and (5) all investors have the same information as management have about the firm's future investment opportunities.

Modigliani and Miller posited their arguments as Proposition I and Proposition II. Simply stated:

Proposition I:

$V_j = D_j + E_j = X_j/P_k$ .... (1A)

or, alternatively:

$P_k = X_j/V_j$ for any firm j in class k ....(1B)

Where V_j measures the value of firm j (j = 1,2 ...), D stands for the value of debt, E stands for the value of equity capital, X is the net return of firm J before interest payments (i.e., EBIT), and P is the cost of equity capital for an all-equity firm (i.e., the rate of capitalization), which is constant for all firms in the given class. Proposition I means *"the market value of any firm is independent of its capital structure and is given by capitalizing its expected return at the rate P appropriate to its class."*

Modigliani and Miller's Proposition II states:

Proposition II:

$i_j - = P + (P - r)D_j/E_j$ .... (2)

where r is the interest rate on debt. Proposition II simply means, *"the market value of any firm is independent of its capital structure and is given by capitalizing its expected return at the rate P appropriate to its class, plus a premium related to financial risk equal to the debt-to-equity ratio times the spread between P and r."*

The two MM "invariance" propositions state that the increase in debt in capital structure will not enhance the value of the firm because the advantage of cheaper debt will be exactly offset by the increase in the cost of equity. Thus, according to Modigliani and Miller, in a world without taxes, both the value of a firm and its cost of capital are unaffected by its capital structure. As proof, MM provided an arbitrage proof to support their propositions. Simply stated, they showed that, under their assumptions, if the two companies differ principally (1) in the way they are financed, and (2) in their total market value, then investors would sell their shares to the overvalued firms, and with those proceeds buy shares of the undervalued firms, and would continue the process until the two companies would have exactly the same market value.

It is to be noted that $V_j = X_j/P_k$ rests on the fact that the net return X_j is a perpetually constant value. In his criticism, Durant (1959) has observed, "indeed, MM's approach to the cost of capital, as the ratio of current earnings to market price, is essentially static," and he had further observed that, "the concept of an equilibrium return class, derived from the notion of static equilibrium, is not adequate to a highly dynamic economy." It is to be noted that in their correction paper (1963), MM had alluded that X can be perpetually constant in a steady-state equilibrium, and therefore, this criticism is moot.

Stiglitz (1969) and Altman (1984) posited that more debt would increase stockholders' and creditors' risk in a firm. Both effects would put an effective limit to a firm's debt-to-equity ratio. But the main criticisms of the MM theorems were their unrealistic assumptions. Realizing this, MM in their 1963 article relaxed the most important objection, i.e., lack of income taxes, particularly corporate taxes. With corporate income taxes, MM concluded that leverage will increase a firm's value because interest payment is tax-deductible, while the dividend income from owning stocks is not. To them, the difference between the levered firm and unlevered firm is that for the former, we have to include any "side effects," such as tax shield:

$$V_L = V_U + TD \quad \text{(3)}$$

Here Magginson (1997 explained the situation with a simple example of two firms, U and L, with a market value of assets worth \$100,000, where firm U financed its assets fully with equity and firm L used 50 percent equity and 50 percent debt, comprising a debt-to-total capital ratio of 50 percent. Each firm generates \$1000,000 in net operating income each year, all of which goes to the shareholders of firm U. Firm L, however, must pay \$30,000 in interest on its debt (\$500,000 with a 6 percent interest rate), leaving \$70,000 for firm L's shareholders. Now, if we introduce a tax on corporate profit at a rate of 35 percent (T = 0.35), this will reduce \$350,000 in the market value of the all-equity company, firm U. For firm L, we can compute the present value of the interest tax shields to be 0.35 x \$500,000 = \$175,000 (this is equal to the tax rate times the amount of interest paid T x rD). Hence, if a 50 percent debt-to-capital ratio firm increases its value by \$175,000 over that of an otherwise equivalent unlevered firm, and each additional \$1 debt increases firm value by 35 cents (corporate tax rate), then the optimal debt-asset ratio should be 100 percent! This is the conclusion we can deduce from the MM 1963 article, which initially made the acceptance of their position less appealing.

The Miller Model

Fourteen years after their correction paper (1963), Professor Miller (1977) alone had introduced the personal income tax to the MM theorems, along with the corporate income tax added earlier. He provided the following formula for the gains from using leverage, G_L, for the stockholders, in a firm holding real assets.

Miller has argued that firms in the aggregate would issue debt and equity in such a way that the before-tax returns on corporate securities and the personal tax rates of the investors would adjust continuously until an equilibrium is obtained. At the equilibrium, $(1 - T_{PS})$ would be equal to $(1 - T_C)(1 - T_{PS})$, and therefore, the tax advantage of issuing debt would be exactly offset by personal taxation. Thus, capital structure is again irrelevant to a firm's value or its cost of capital. Any situation in which the owners of corporations could increase their wealth by substituting debt for equity (or vice versa) would be incompatible with market equilibrium.

Some of the criticisms of both the MM theorems and the Miller model are that they assume corporate and personal leverage to be perfect substitutes. But in reality they are not, because if a person invests in corporate stocks, he or she will have limited liability while for personal investments he or she will face unlimited liability, even using the "homemade" leverage. This additional risk may retard individuals from using arbitrage activities, so that the equilibrium conditions MM have posited would be different in reality. Also, institutional investors face many governmental restrictions that would inhibit their ability to use homemade leverage.

Second, if an unlevered firm faces financial losses, it would cut dividends, rather than taking the shelter of the bankruptcy court. If the dividend is cut, then the individuals using homemade leverage will have less money. This will put them in greater financial distress than the stockholders of levered firms.

Third, MM argue that both corporations and individuals may borrow at the same rate. But in reality, corporations generally borrow at a "privilaged" (i.e. lower) rate, while most of the individuals pay a higher rate than corporations.

Fourth, Miller assumes that the tax benefits from corporate debt would be the same for firms of all sizes. But again, in reality larger firms gain more from increased leverage than smaller, financially burdened firms. Also, larger firms may have other non-debt tax shields such as depletion allowances, higher depreciation, and larger pension plan contributions, that smaller firms may not have.

Finally, MM, and Miller especially, do not take into account the effect of brokerage fees and transaction costs that in reality, most of the individuals as well as corporations have to face. They do not discuss the costs of financial distress, agency costs, costs associated with information asymmetry and so forth. While the Modigliani-Miller model is the first step toward constructing a capital structure theory, other factors have to be taken into account to make it a guide to corporate decision making.

Optimal Capital Structure Theory

The introduction of corporate and personal income taxes to the Modigliani-Miller theorems still leaves out other imperfections in the capital market such as bankruptcy costs and financial distress. The famous article by DeAngelo and Masulis (1980) on optimal capital structure, incorporates such bankruptcy costs explicitly. In their model, regardless of whether default costs are large or small, the market's relative prices of debt and equity will adjust in such a way that the net (corporate and marginal personal) tax advantage of debt is of the same magnitude as expected marginal default costs. The relative prices will equilibrate in this way to induce firms to supply the proper quantities of debt and equity to satisfy the demand of investors. In particular, the presence of non-debt tax shields and/or default costs implies optimum leverage ratio for each firm.

The bankruptcy costs of firms with increasing leverage can better be expressed by the costs associated with increasing financial distress. But as Gilson, John, and Lang (1990) have pointed out, costs associated with bankruptcy and financial distress will discourage the use of financial leverage only if (1) financial distress would reduce market demand for a firm's products or increase its cost of production; (2) financial distress would give the firm's managers operating or financial incentives to act in such a way as to reduce the value of the firm; or (3) entering bankruptcy would impose deadweight costs to the firm involved.

A firm's asset characteristics also will influence its use of the degree of leverage in its capital structure, i.e., costs of distress vary with types of assets. Companies whose assets are mostly tangible and have a well-developed secondary market will have less fear of financial distress than companies having more intangible assets. Also, companies that are more involved in research and development activities will have more sunk costs, and therefore, will be more prone to financial distress. Companies which are perceived as too risky may also have problems with suppliers and production costs, and thus subject to greater costs of financial distress than otherwise. Finally, the chance that a firm will become bankrupt due to its inability to meet its obligations to its creditors depends to a large extent on its level of both business risk and financial risk.

The seminal article by Jensen and Mackling (1976) has brought forth the Agency Cost theory of capital structure. Here not only have they viewed firms as an interaction between the principals (shareholders) and agents (managers) involving agency costs, but also between lenders and borrowers incurring agency costs. A firm with an all-equity capital structure will substitute bonds for stocks in order to reduce the agency cost of equity. But with greater bond issues, bondholders may lose out at the cost of stockholders. This cost of lost efficiency plus monitoring costs for debt issues are what is meant by the term "agency costs," and the existence of these costs increases the cost of leverage to the firm.

We can now tie together the modern Agency Cost/Tax Shield approach to corporate financial literature. The equation below expresses the value of a levered firm in terms of the value of an unlevered firm, adjusted for the present value of tax shields, bankruptcy costs, and the agency costs of debt and equity:

$V_L = V_U$ + PV of tax shields – PV of bankruptcy costs – PV Agency Costs of Equity – PV Agency Costs of Debt .... (4)

We can express this relationship in Figure 1.1 where the value of the firm is maximized when the weighted average cost of capital is minimized. The after-tax cost of debt, $K_D(1 - T_C)$ is low at first due to the tax deductibility of interest payments, and slowly rises with increasing leverage to compensate the bondholders for increasing risk. The cost of equity, K_S , is above the cost of debt and would increase at a rapid pace with increasing leverage, because the stockholders would require higher returns for the higher financial risk associated with greater leverage. The weighted average cost of capital, K_A (= WACC), will decrease at first with

Figure 1.1

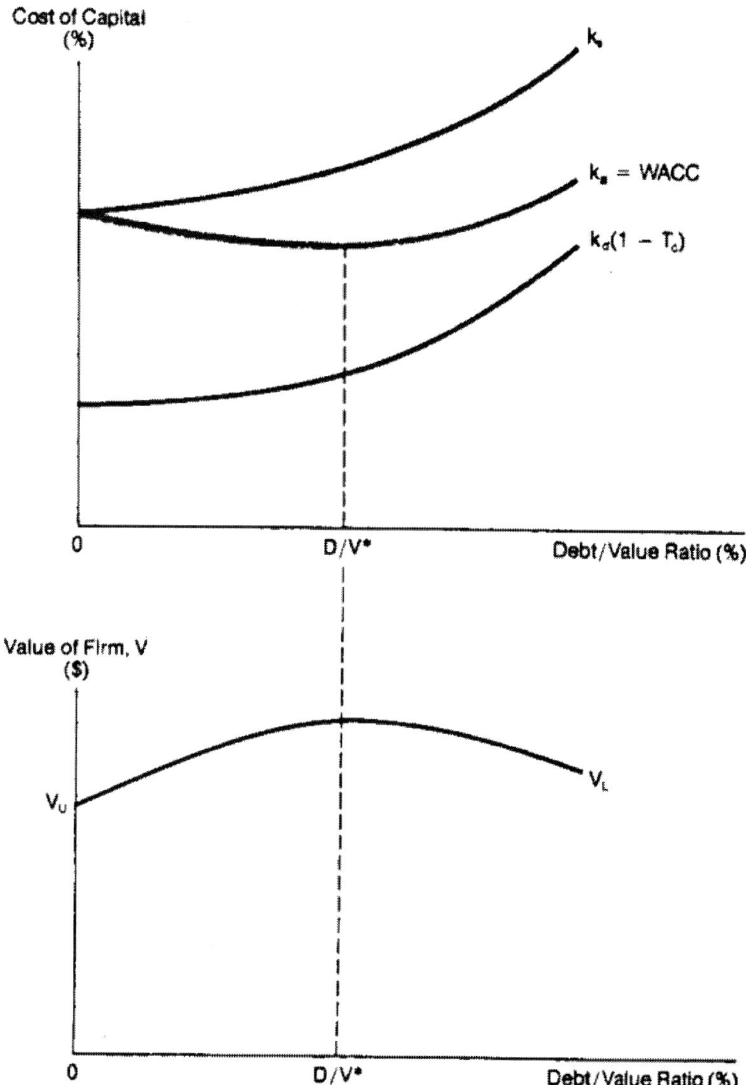

lower debt cost, will reach its lowest point, and then will start to climb up as both the costs of equity and debt begin to rise again.

This is the standard optimal capital structure theory of the trade-off model. As the bottom part of the diagram shows, the value of the levered firm, V_L, will start to rise as the debt ratio increases and as the weighted average cost of capital declines, and will reach its highest point before starting to fall back when the WACC begins to rise again. D/V* is the point where the debt-equity ratio reaches its optimal value.

According to the optimal capital structure theory, companies have a target debt-equity ratio they strive to reach. Of course, the target debt ratio will vary from firm to firm. Companies with high tangible assets and tax-shield interest income would have high target ratios, while unprofitable firms with risky, intangible assets will have low target debt ratios. But this theory's main deficiency is that the most profitable companies generally borrow the least even though they should have a high target debt ratio. This is a static trade-off theory of optimal capital structure, which does not take into account the realities of the capital markets, such as the aggressive use of debt in leverage buyouts (LBO), hostile takeovers, and restructuring, and the use of debt as a signal for higher values of the firm. Also, the trade-off theory does not explain the inverse relationship found in many studies between leverage and profitability. The trade-off theory would predict just the opposite—higher profits mean more savings from interest tax-shields. This should mean higher target-debt ratios, yet in reality it is just the opposite.

Richard Castenias (1983) tested the optimal capital structure theory by examining the time trend of several key capital structure ratios, i.e., whether they are increasing or decreasing over time. He had shown that the ratios exhibited the following trends:

Following the optimal capital structure hypothesis, we would expect the ratio of long-term debt to total assets (LTD/TA) as the risk of bankruptcy becomes more important. Similarly, under the optimal capital structure theory, the ratio of long-term debt to net worth (LTD/NW) would decrease over time, as would the ratio of long-term debt to total capital (LTD/TC), and long-term debt to net worth (LTD/NW). Since the assets of a successful company should generate more and more net worth, we would expect the ratio of net worth to total assets (NW/TA) to increase over time. Finally, a successful company should also generate higher cash flows, so that the ratio of cash flow to long-term debt (CF/LTD) would also increase over time.

Financial Ratios Signs of Optimal Capital Structure

LTD/TA	Decreasing over Time
LTD/NW	Decreasing over Time
LTD/TC	Decreasing over Time
TL/NW	Decreasing over Time
NW/TA	Increasing over Time
CF/LTD	Increasing over Time

The Signaling Effects and Asymmetric Information

In the late 1970s, Ross (1977) and Leland and Pyle (1977) developed a signaling model of capital structure based on asymmetric information problems between well-informed managers of a firm and the poorly-informed outside stockholders. This theory suggests that managers of well-developed corporations are privy to better information about the prospects of their firms and are willing to share that information with their shareholders and prospective investors. But if they simply announce that good news, managers of other firms can do the same and in that case the investing public will be skeptical about the veracity of the information. So the managers of the firms with good prospects have to give a signal to the investors, which comes in the way of issuing debt instead of issuing equity.

According to the proponents of this theory, issuing bonds in the capital market gives a positive signal that the stock is undervalued and the management wants to share the higher future profits with the existing stockholders. But issuing new stocks gives a negative signal to the effect that the stock is overvalued and the company has poor growth prospects, and wants to pass the burden to the new stockholders. Thus an increase in leverage will enhance the price of the firm's stock and, hence, raise the value of the firm, while increasing the issuance of stock will lower the price of the stock of the company and, thus, lower the value of the firm. Given this reasoning, a separating equilibrium occurs where high-value firms use more debt in their capital structures, while low-value firms resort to more equity financing. Since the low-value firms are unwilling to follow the path of high-value firms, the equilibrium is stable.

The signaling theory, although intuitively appealing, is, unfortunately, a poor provider of actual behavior. For example, this theory suggests that an increase in leverage will lead to higher profits, but actually almost all the research papers on the subject have found an inverse relationship with leverage ratios and profitability. Moreover, this theory would suggest that newer firms with high growth prospects and intangible assets should employ more debt than equity, while in reality the mature firms with high tangible assets use relatively more debt in their capital structures. We should remember that the signaling model has not been developed as well as other competing theories, and much more room remains in the future for further refinement of the theory.

But Ross's article brought forth in the finance literature the problems associated with asymmetric information in the capital market, which

Professor Stewart Myers (1984) developed more fully later on. Myers had found that the homogeneous expectations by investors are not true and the asymmetric (i.e., different) information by different groups of market participants are the general norm. For example, the capital market perceives that managers know more about the firm than outside shareholders. That is why the market reacts to earnings announcements, major investments, or stock repurchases of the firms accordingly. Also, the case studies analyzed by Professor Donaldson (1984) showed that the majority of the firms in the United States used internal financing more than external financing. From all these facts Myers (1984) and Myers and Majluf (1984), developed the Pecking Order Theory—that firms first use their retained earnings (internal financing), and if external financing is needed, debt financing is used first, and finally, common stock is issued. Their arguments were reinforced by Asquith and Mullins (1986), Mickelson and Parch (1986), and Shyam-Sunder and Myers (1999).

The Pecking Order Theory

We can express the Pecking Order Theory in Myers' own words:

1. Firms prefer internal finance.
2. They adopt their target dividend payout ratios to their investment opportunities, while trying to avoid sudden changes in dividends.
3. Sticky dividend policies, plus unpredictable fluctuations in profitability and investment opportunities, mean that internally generated cash flow is sometimes more than capital expenditures and at other times less. If it is more, the firm pays off debt or invests in marketable securities. If it is less, the firm first draws down its cash balance or sells its marketable securities.
4. If external finance is required, firms issue the safest security first. That is, they start with debt, then possibly hybrid securities such as convertible bonds, then perhaps equity as a last resort.

In the traditional trade-off theory, there is a target debt ratio which the firms are striving to achieve in the long run (Taggart (1985), Jalilvand and Harris (1984), and Auerback (1985)). But in the pecking order theory there is no such thing, and the firms make debt ratio changes when there is a surplus or deficit in the internal cash flows and real investment opportunities. Profitable firms will generally have a low debt ratio and will borrow only when investments exceed internal cash flows. Given the stickiness of the dividend payout ratio, less profitable firms will have less internal funds to invest and will borrow to finance investments. A firm with negative profits will have no internally-generated funds and will entirely depend on external debt and equity to avail itself of any investment opportunities.

The pecking order theory arises out of the asymmetric information between the managers and the stockholders we find in the capital market today. According to Myers, it has three immediate implications. First, internal equity is better than external equity because excess operating cash flows can be used automatically and their use does not convey any information to the investors. Second, financial slack is valuable. Financial slack is the sum of cash, marketable securities, and readily saleable real assets. When an investment opportunity arises, a firm rich in liquid assets can convert them into investable funds quickly, without going to the bond market or having to sell equity at a discounted price. Third, debt is better than equity if external financing is required because debt is safer than equity and will be affected less by asymmetric information problems. Thus, issuing safer securities minimize managers' information advantage as the managers cannot play with overvalued or undervalued equities.

Myers himself had admitted that, in practice, the pecking order theory cannot be wholly right. For a variety of reasons, firms many times issue equity when they could issue debt. But it explains better the strong inverse relationship between leverage and profitability, which the trade-off theory cannot. It also explains better why stock prices fall when the company issues equity. The announcement of an equity issue is usually considered bad news because investors think that managers have better information and issue equity only when it is overvalued. Similarly, exchanging debt for equity is considered good news because their decision to repurchase equity generated optimism and pushes stock prices up.

The pecking order theory assumes that managers work in the interest of the existing stockholders, maximizing the value of their stock. But the theory does not say why they will be concerned with the over-valued or under-valued of their stock, barring the compensation package incentive worked out in Ross's signaling model. As Dybvig and Zender (1991) have pointed out, there are alternative models that will reach the same predictions as the pecking order theory with managerial compensation embedded to determine the choice of debt and equity decisions.

The conclusions of the pecking order theory belie reality, as Fama and French (1998) have pointed out. They analyzed a sample of firms for NYSE, AMEX and Nasdaq exchanges from 1973 to 2002. They found that the annual percentage of firms issuing stock has increased from 54 percent during 1973-1982 to 62 percent in 1983-1992, and reached 72 percent during 1993-2002. To Fama and French, the main reasons for the failure of the pecking order theory are due to issuing stocks with low transaction costs and problems relating to asymmetric information.

In some cases, there seems to be a relation between capital structure decisions and the occurrence of good opportunities to issue securities such as cases of market euphoria. Here Baker and Jeffrey (2001) suggest that firms with less financial leverage are those who obtained more equity when their prices were high. Loughran and Ritter (1997) showed that firms that issued stocks in moments of market euphoria had bad financial results afterwards, because issues were not motivated by the existence of better investment opportunities, but to take advantage of rising stock prices. This suggests that public issues of shares would be an alternative for firms with bad financial results or prospects in moments of market euphoria. Brav and Gompers (1997) show that the increase in liquidity and information efficiency of public capital markets call for investors' attention. This is in tune with the increase in the number of initial public offerings (IPOs) in phases of greater market liquidity.

We have thus seen the modern capital structure theory boils down to this: a comparison between the optimal capital structure theory and the pecking order theory. Both are conditional theories and one works better in some conditions and circumstances than the other. Both have their strong and weak points and both are amenable to sophisticated statistical tests. That should be our prime objective which we intend to pursue in the next chapter.

References

Altman, E., 1984, "A Further Empirical Investigation of the Bankruptcy Cost Questions," *Journal of Finance* 39, 1067-1089.

Asquith, P. and D. W. Mullins, 1986, "Equity Issues and Offering Dilution," *Journal of Financial Economics* 15, 61-89.

Auerback, A., 1985, "Real Determinants of Corporate Leverage," in B. M. Friedman, ed. *Corporate Capital Structures in the United States*, Chicago: University of Chicago Press, 301-24.

Baker, M. P. and W. Jeffrey, 2001, "Market Timing and Capital Structure," Yale International Center for Finance, *Working Paper*, No. 00-32.

Barclay, M. J., C. W. Smith, Jr., and R. W. Watts, 1995, "The Determinants of Corporate Leverage and Dividend Policies," *Journal of Applied Corporate Finance* 7, 4-19.

_______________, 1999, "The Capital Structure Puzzle: Another Look at the Evidence, " *Journal of Applied Corporate Finance* 12, 8-20.

Baskin, J., 1989, "An Empirical Examination of the Pecking Order Hypothesis," *Financial Management* 18, 26-35.

Brealey, R. A. and S. C. Myers, 2000, *Principles of Corporate Finance*, New York: McGraw-Hill.

Brav A. and P. A. Gompers, 1997, "Myth or Reality: The Long Run Under-Performance of Initial Public Offerings: Evidence from Venture and Non-venture Capital–Backed Companies," *Journal of Finance* 52, 1791-1822.

Castenias, R., 1983, "Bankruptcy Risk and Optimal Capital Structure," *Journal of Finance* 38, 1617-1635.

DeAngelo, H. and R. W. Masulis, 1980, "Optimal Capital Structure under Corporate and Personal Taxation," *Journal of Financial Economics* 8, 3-30.

Donaldson, G., 1984, *Managing Corporate Wealth: The Operation of a Comprehensive Financial Goal System*, New York: Praeger.

Durant, D., 1959, "The Cost of Debt and Equity Funds for Businesses," in E. Solomon, Ed., *The Management of Corporate Capital*, New York: Free Press.

________, 1959, "The Cost of Capital, Corporation Finance and the Theory of Investment: Comment," *American Economic Review* 49, 639-655.

Dybvig, P. and J. F. Zender, 1991, "Capital Structure and Dividend Irrelevance with Asymmetric Information," *Review of Financial Studies* 4, 201-19.

Fama, E., 1978, "The Effects of a Firm's Financing and Investment Decisions on the Welfare of its Security Holders," *American Economic Review* 68, 274-284.

Fama, E. and K. R. French, 1998, "Taxes, Financing Decisions, and Firm Value," *Journal of Finance* 53, 819-43.

________________________, 2003, "Financing Decision: Who Issue Stocks?" CRSP *Working Paper*, No. 549.

Gilson, S. C., K. John, and L. H. P. Lang, "Troubled Debt Restructurings: An Empirical Study of Private Reorganization of Firms in Default," *Journal of Financial Economics* 27, 315-353.

Harris, M. and A. Raviv, 1991, "The Theory of Capital Structure," *Journal of Finance* 46, 297-355.

Jalilvand, A. and R. S. Harris, 1984, "Corporate Behavior in Adjusting to Capital Structure and Dividend Targets: An Econometric Study," *Journal of Finance* 39, 127-144.

Jensen, M. C. and W. H. Mackling, 1976, "Theory of the Firm: Managerial Behavior, Agency Costs, and Ownership Structure," *Journal of Financial Economics* 3, 305-360.

Loughran, T. and J. R. Ritter, 1997, "Ownership Structure: Conducting Seasoned Equity Offerings," *Journal of Finance* 52, 1823-1850.

Leland, H. and D. Pyle, 1977, "Information Asymmetries, Financial Structure, and Financial Intermediation," *Journal of Finance* 32, 371-387.

Magginson, W. L., 1997, *Corporate Finance Theory*, Springfield, MA: Addison-Wesley, Chapter 7.

Mickelson, W. and M. M. Partch, 1986, "Valuation Effects of Security Offerings and the Issuance Process," *Journal of Financial Economics* 15, 31-60.

Miller, M., 1977, "Death and Taxes," *Journal of Finance* 32, 261-276.

________, 1989, "The Modigliani-Miller Propositions After Thirty Years," *Journal of Applied Corporate Finance* 2, 6-18.

Modigliani, F. and M. Miller, 1958, "The Cost of Capital, Corporate Finance, and the Theory of Investments," *American Economic Review* 48, 261-297.

__________________________, 1963, "Corporate Income Taxes and the Cost of Capital: A Correction," *American Economic Review* 53, 433-443.

Myers, S. C., 1984, "The Capital Structure Puzzle," *Journal of Finance* 39, 575-592

__________, 1993, "Still Searching for Optimal Capital Structure," *Journal of Applied Corporate Finance* 1, 4-14.

__________, 2001, "Capital Structure," *Journal of Economic Perspectives* 15, 81-102.

______ and N. S. Majluf, 1984, "Corporate Financing and Investment Decisions When Firms Have Information Investors Do Not Have," *Journal of Financial Economics* 43, 187-221.

Rajan, R. G. and L. Zingales, 1995, "What Do We Know about Capital Structure? Some Evidence from International Data," *Journal of Finance* 50, 1421-1460.
Ross, S. A., 1977, "The Determination of Financial Structure: The Incentive-Signaling Approach," *Bell Journal of Economics* 8, 23-40.
Shyam-Sunder, L. and S. C. Myers, 1999, "Testing Static Trade Off Against Pecking Order Model of Capital Structure, *Journal of Financial Economics* 51, 219-44.
Solomon, E., Ed., 1959, *The Management of Corporate Capital*, New York: Free Press.
Stiglitz, J. E., 1969, "A Reexamination of the Modigliani-Miller Theorem," *American Economic Review* 54, 784-793.
Taggart, Jr., R. A., 1985, "Secular Patterns in the Financing of U.S. Corporations," in B. M. Friedman (Ed.), *Corporate Capital Structures in the United States,* Chicago: University of Chicago Press.
Wald, J. K., 1999, "How Firm Characteristics Affect Capital Structure," *Journal of Financial Research* 22, 161-87.
Zingales, L,2000, "In Search of New Foundations, *Journal of Finance* 55, 1623-53.

2

Capital Structure: Tests of Optimality vs. Pecking Order Theory

Introduction

The optimal capital structure theory evolved through the writings of Franco Modigliani and Merton Miller (MM, 1958). At first they proposed that, in a world of no income taxes and transaction costs, a firm's capital structure is irrelevant to its value. But with the introduction of corporation income taxes and transaction costs (MM, 1963), it was proposed that a firm would use its debt financing judiciously so that its tax shelter would balance its chance of potential bankruptcy. Hence the evolution of the notion of optimal capital structure where the debt/equity mix would be such that the firm's weighted average cost of capital would be minimized and its value would be maximized. DeAngelo and Masulis in their famous 1980 article had articulated it in such a way that the proposition came to be known as the "optimal capital structure."

In 1982 Bowen, Daley and Huber, Jr. (BDH) had provided a technique by which we can test the optimal capital structure. They proposed that an individual firm's debt structure tends to converge to its industry mean over time. Marsh (1982) had concluded that "companies do appear to make the choice of financing instrument as though they had target levels in mind for both long-term debt ratios and the ratio of short-term to total debt." Stewart Myers in his seminal article (1984) had proposed the pecking order theory (POT)—that firms choose internal capital at first, i.e., the use of retained earnings. When external capital is needed, they choose debt capital, and then equity capital as the last resort. Taggart (1986) used POT in his study of capital structure and found that the pecking order hypothesis was more valid than the optimal capital structure hypothesis.

More recently, E. T. Claggett, Jr. (1992) tested the optimal capital structure theory and had found that long-term debt to total assets ratio, for the most part, tended to move toward the most recent previous industry mean within one year. In general, in more firms with above the industry mean long-term debt ratios adjusted toward the industry mean than with below the industry mean ratios. Claggett, Jr. also found that firms normally behave in a manner consistent with the pecking order theory, but some firms may not adjust during periods of severe turmoil.

Ghosh and Cai (1999) previously had tested both the optimal capital structure hypothesis and pecking order hypothesis and found that firms would adjust their capital structure toward the industry mean when it was above the mean, but that firms below the industry mean would adjust their capital structure toward the industry mean rather sluggishly. But that study had also shown that both the optimal capital structure hypothesis and the pecking order hypothesis coexisted during the period covered by our study (1974-1992). In that article, the data used were collected from *Fortune* magazine's largest 500 United States companies. Here we will test the two hypotheses anew with the help of the *COMPUSTAT* database. Also, we will advance the years from 1983 to 2001 in order to take up the more recent time period of the United States industries.

Methodological Framework

To test the optimal capital structure theory we have employed two methodologies in this paper. The first methodology we have pursued here was introduced by BDH first and later refined by E. T. Claggett, Jr. where a two-by-two contingency table was formulated. The nonparametric Fisher Exact Probability (FEP) test and later the Goodman-Kruskal Gamma measures were employed to analyze the data. To examine whether firms converge their capital structure toward their industry mean, the two-by-two matrix was analyzed for each year (across industry) and each industry (across year) in the following manner: the hypothesis tested by this procedure is that gamma is significantly different from zero. If there is no statistical significance we conclude that there is no discernable trend to move toward or away from the industry mean capital structure. The results are shown in tables 2.1 through 2.4.

To examine whether firms move (converge) their capital structure toward their industry's mean, a two-by-two matrix was analyzed for each year (across industry), for each industry (across year), and for all observations (pooled across both industries and years). Figure 2.1 describes the following matrix:

Figure 2.1

Number of Firms below (L) that did correct	Number of Firms below (L) that did not correct
Number of Firms above (L) that did not correct	Number of Firms above (L) that did correct

For the statistical calculations, following Claggett, Jr., we have estimated Gamma for the Goodman-Kruskal gamma measure and the associated test statistic (Z) were also calculated. The hypothesis tested by this procedure is that gamma is significantly different than zero. If there is no statistical significance, we conclude that there is no discernable trend to move toward or away from the industry mean capital structure. The results are shown in tables 2.1 and 2.2.

If there is convergence (or divergence), an analysis of a similar but different two-by-two matrix determines whether the movement was by firms from both sides of (symmetric), by firms below (asymmetric), or by firms above (asymmetric) of their industry mean LTD/TA ratios. The matrix is described below by figure 2.2:

Figure 2.2

Number of Firms below (L) that did correct	Number of Firms below (L) That did correct
Number of Firms above (H) that did not correct	Number of Firms above (H) That did not correct

For each figure 2 x 2 (2 by 2) matrix, an estimate of G and associated test statistic (Z) were calculated. The hypothesis, again, is that G is significantly different than zero. If there is significance with convergence and the sign of G is positive (+), the conclusion is that the movement was by those firms with the measurement ratios below the industry means, and vice versa if the sign is negative (-). The results are shown in tables 2.3 and 2.4.

To test the POT, a two-by-four matrix was analyzed for each industry (across year), for each year (across industry), and for all observations pooled. Figure 2.3 describes the matrix:

Figure 2.3

Number of firms below (L) that were passive (P)	Number of firms below (L) that issued debt (D)	Number of firms below (L) that issued equity(E)	Number of firms below (L) that issued both (B)
Number of firms above (H) that were passive(P)	Number of firms above (H) that issued debt (D)	Number of firms above (H) that issued equity(E)	Number of firms above (H) that issued both (B)

For each figure 2.3 matrix, an estimate of G and the associated test statistic (Z) were calculated. Here the hypothesis is that G is significantly different from zero. If there is no significance, we conclude that there is no support for Pecking Order Theory. But if G is significant and the sign is positive (+), we will interpret that as a corroboration of the POT. The result is shown in table 2.5 and 2.6.

Empirical Results

In table 2.1, we find that for the measure of LTD/TA, eighteen out of the twenty-one industries had Z statistics that were positive and significant either at the 0.01 percent or 0.05 percent level (two-tail test). For the measure of TD/TA, nineteen industries had significant Z statistics, while for the measure of TE/TA, nineteen industries also had significant Z statistics either at the 0.01 percent or 0.05 percent level. The pooled data also shows this tendency toward convergence when the Z statistics for all of the three measures were significant at the 0.01 percent level. These results strongly indicate that firms do converge toward their respective industry mean, thus supporting the optimal capital structure hypothesis.

Table 2.2 shows the convergence toward the industry mean within one year. Here, for the LTD/TA measure of capital structure the Z statistics were significant in seventeen out of nineteen years, either at the 0.01 percent or 0.05 percent level. But for the TD/TA measure of capital structure, the Z statistics were significant only in ten out of nineteen years.

However, the results were much better for the industry convergence when TE/TA measure was taken into account. Here the Z statistics were significant in fourteen out of nineteen years. The pooled data were also significant at the 0.01 percent level for all the three measures of capital structure. Thus both tables 2.1 and 2.2 support the conclusions reached by Jalilvand and Harris (1984), Lev (1969), Marsh (1982), and Claggett, Jr. (1992), but not by BDH (1982), where they found no significant convergence over one-year intervals.

Table 2.1
Summary of Capital Structure Symmetric Convergence, By Industry1983-2001
LTD/TA—Long-term debt over total assets; TD/TA—Total debt over total assets; TE/TA—Total equity over total assets.

		LTD/TA		TD/TA		TE/TA	
Industry	Obs.	Gamma	Z-Test	Gamma	Z-Test	Gamma	Z-Test
Aerospace	290	0.138	1.675	.339	4.339**	.357	4.598**
Apparel	780	0.532	12.393**	.133	2.660**	.575	13.89**
Beverage	123	0.577	5.538**	.260	2.111*	0.261	2.124*
Building Materials	117	0.317	2.560*	.208	1.630	0.088	0.677
Chemicals	258	0.416	5.201**	.371	4.534**	0.288	3.421**
Computers, Office Equip.	243	0.518	6.669**	.368	4.360**	0.494	6.270**
Electronics, Elec. Equip.	454	0.391	6.409**	.364	5.892**	0.444	7.470**
Food	345	0.424	6.148**	.418	6.038**	0.463	6.852**
Forest Products	389	0.497	7.980**	.425	6.545**	0.569	9.654**
Industrial & Farm Equip.	260	0.250	2.938**	.332	4.012**	0.245	2.880**
Metal Products	224	0.395	4.551**	.248	2.711**	0.292	3.235**
Metals	290	0.015	0.176	.426	5.670**	0.366	4.733**
Mining, Crude oil Prod.	130	0.302	2.555*	.553	5.351**	0.436	3.906**
Motor Vehicles & Parts	356	0.246	3.384**	.424	6.240**	0.201	2.736**
Petroleum Refining	987	0.266	6.127**	.360	8.567**	0.346	8.189**
Pharmaceuticals	330	0.520	7.823**	.478	6.981**	0.610	9.901**
Publishing, Printing	458	0.423	7.070**	.400	6.597**	0.488	8.469**
Sci. & Photo Equip.	232	0.394	4.615**	.406	4.787**	0.377	4.385**
Soaps, Cosmetics	267	0.509	6.836**	.460	5.985**	0.325	3.967**
Textile	126	0.167	1.340	.040	0.317	0.171	1.378
Tobacco	114	0.355	2.867**	.040	0.300	0.370	3.003**
Total	6773	0.309	18.903**	0.391	24.743**	0.398	25.22**

* Significant at the 5% level.
** Significant at the 1% level.

In table 2.3, we have shown the summary of asymmetric convergence by industry during 1983-2001. This table strongly corroborates the conclusion of table 2.1 that the majority of firms had converged their LTD/TD ratios toward their industry means. Here seventeen out of twenty-one industries had convergence with the Z statistics either at the 0.01 percent or at the 0.05 percent level of significance, while for the measure of TD/TA, twelve industries had convergence with the Z statistics significant either at the 0.01 percent or 0.05 percent level of significance. But in the case of TE/TA ratio, only six industries had convergence either at the 0.01 percent or 0.05 percent level of significance. Also, in the majority of industries the negative signs of the Z statistics

Table 2.2
Summary of Capital Structure Symmetric Convergence, By Year 1983-2001 LTD/TA—(Long-term debt over total assets); TD/TA—(Total debt over total assets); TE/TA—(Total equity over total assets).

		LTD/TA		TD/TA		TE/TA	
Year	Obs.	Gamma	Z-Test	Gamma	Z-Test	Gamma	Z-Test
1983	297	0.368	4.822**	0.358	4.667**	0.312	4.005**
1984	314	0.326	4.321**	0.301	3.953**	0.281	3.669**
1985	318	0.199	2.567*	0.194	2.491*	0.336	4.501**
1986	320	0.225	2.915**	0.140	1.785	0.149	1.911
1987	321	0.214	2.779**	0.082	1.048	0.202	2.614**
1988	332	0.396	5.550**	0.094	1.222	0.096	1.243
1989	334	0.140	1.833	0.099	1.280	0.168	2.203*
1990	350	0.369	5.245**	0.134	1.784	0.019	0.252
1991	352	0.201	2.722**	0.219	2.976**	0.034	0.453
1992	353	0.405	5.880**	0.322	4.518**	0.276	3.811**
1993	360	0.122	1.650	0.098	1.325	0.203	2.776**
1994	371	0.194	2.690**	0.110	1.507	0.185	2.568*
1995	379	0.941	38.408**	0.003	0.043	0.151	2.108*
1996	384	0.357	5.287**	0.283	4.087**	0.410	6.230**
1997	384	0.255	3.657**	0.948	41.442**	0.986	80.95**
1998	395	0.183	2.621**	0.147	2.082*	0.315	4.670**
1999	398	0.139	1.985*	0.121	1.726	0.286	4.208**
2000	400	0.201	2.908**	0.153	2.192*	0.124	1.774
2001	411	0.299	4.484**	0.219	3.224**	0.373	5.758**
Total	6773	0.309	18.903**	0.391	24.743**	0.398	25.22**

* Significant at the 5% level.
** Significant at the 1% level.

meant that the convergence came from above. This again supports the results obtained by Claggett, Jr. (1992), that the convergence toward the industry mean came most often from firms above their industry mean LTD/TA ratios. The pooled data for all these measures of capital structure also confirms the result of convergence that were significant at the 0.01 percent level of significance.

In table 2.4 we have calculated the gamma values and the Z statistics for the asymmetric convergence by year. We find that the Z statistics were significant in fourteen out of nineteen years for the LTD/TA measure, while for both the TD/TA and TE/TA measures, eleven out of nineteen years had the Z statistics significant either at the 0.01 percent or 0.05 percent level of significance. Also, the negative signs for the majority of years (except for the TE/TA measure, meant that the convergence movement came from above, as seen in the case of the majority of

Table 2.3
Summary of Capital Structure Asymmetric Convergence, By Industry 1983-2001
LTD/TA—Long-term debt over total assets; TD/TA—Total debt over total assets; TE/TA—Total equity over total assets.

		LTD/TA		TD/TA		TE/TA	
Industry	Obs.	Gamma	Z-Test	Gamma	Z-Test	Gamma	Z-Test
Aerospace	290	-0.531	-7.552**	-0.255	-3.181**	-0.140	-1.698
Apparel	780	-0.487	-11.017**	-0.332	-6.945**	0.051	1.003
Beverage	123	0.443	3.870**	-0.062	-0.487	-0.505	-4.589**
Building Materials	117	-0.414	3.474**	0.043	0.330	-0.113	-0.867
Chemicals	258	0.180	2.083*	-0.197	-2.283*	-0.227	-2.642**
Computers, Office Equip.	243	-0.144	-1.602	0.029	0.319	-0.080	-0.882
Electronics, Elec. Equip	454	-0.417	-6.909**	-0.150	-2.293*	0.012	0.178
Food	345	-0.288	-3.949**	-0.167	-2.227	0.008	0.100
Forest Products	389	-0.033	-0.463	-0.011	-0.146	-0.156	-2.206*
Industrial & Farm Equip.	260	-0.224	-2.626**	-0.223	-2.609**	0.065	0.744
Metal Products	224	-0.402	-4.639**	-0.127	-1.358	-0.026	-0.279
Metals	290	-0.448	-6.040**	-0.352	-4.529**	-0.157	-1.911
Mining, Crude oil Prod.	130	-0.175	-1.430	-0.107	-0.871	0.133	1.079
Motor Vehicles & Parts	356	-0.205	-2.797**	-0.231	-3.168**	0.116	1.560
Petroleum Refining	987	-0.288	-6.670**	-0.245	-5.605**	-0.156	-3.513**
Pharmaceuticals	330	-0.559	-8.668**	0.022	0.288	-0.130	-1.679
Publishing, Printing	458	-0.281	-4.422**	-0.184	-2.838**	0.034	0.521
Sci. & Photo Equip.	232	-0.536	-6.833**	-0.153	-1.670	0.263	2.930**
Soaps, Cosmetics	267	0.227	2.698**	0.225	2.666**	0.216	2.557**
Textile	126	-0.443	-3.920**	-0.400	-3.468**	0.122	0.972
Tobacco	114	-0.638	-6.262	0.533	4.760**	0.152	1.164
Total	6773	-0.330	-20.323	0.165	9.714**	0.081	4.740**

* Significant at the 5% level.
** Significant at the 1% level.

industries. The pooled data for only the LTD/TA measure showed the negative sign, meaning that the convergence toward the industry mean came from the above.

Table 2.5 shows the results for pecking order preference by industry during 1983-2001 for the LTD/TA measure of capital structure. Claggett, Jr. (1992) found strong support for pecking order behavior except for two industries—newspaper publishing and the retail sector. Here we find that all the industries taken in our sample had positive and significant Z-test for their gamma values at the 0.01 percent level of significance. The pooled data also corroborates this result which was highly significant at the 0.01 percent level of significance.

Table 2.4
Summary of Capital Structure Asymmetric Convergence, By Year 1983-2001
LTD/TA—Long-term debt over total assets; TD/TA—Total debt over total assets; TE/TA—Total equity over total assets.

		LTD/TA		TD/TA		TE/TA	
Industry	Obs.	Gamma	Z-Test	Gamma	Z-Test	Gamma	Z-Test
1983	297	-0.200	-2.461*	0.595	8.923**	0.693	11.575**
1984	314	0.171	3.431**	-0.762	-23.25**	0.542	12.724**
1985	318	-0.761	-9.202**	-0.327	-2.712**	0.224	1.799
1986	320	-0.550	-5.034**	-0.277	-2.206*	0.045	0.344
1987	321	0.470	6.046**	-0.257	-3.020	-0.451	-5.739**
1988	332	-0.642	-9.219**	0.026	0.291	-0.359	-4.241**
1989	334	-0.296	-4.671**	-0.199	-3.052**	0.110	1.663
1990	350	-0.509	-7.758**	-0.317	-4.387**	0.132	1.750
1991	352	0.104	1.455	-0.648	-11.861**	0.284	4.124**
1992	353	-0.579	-8.098**	-0.604	-8.645**	-0.257	-3.032**
1993	360	-0.531	-6.637**	-0.081	-0.857	-0.219	-2.374*
1994	371	-0.180	-2.198*	-0.219	-2.707**	-0.291	-3.658**
1995	379	-0.025	-0.200	0.026	0.213	-0.086	-0.693
1996	384	-0.120	-1.609	0.106	1.417	-0.428	-6.312**
1997	384	-0.332	-7.814**	-0.129	-2.893**	-0.094	-2.086*
1998	395	-0.158	-2.057*	-0.145	-1.884	-0.096	-1.239
1999	398	-0.212	-3.280**	0.116	1.766	-0.152	-2.327
2000	400	-0.044	-0.473	-0.303	-3.419**	0.211	2.322*
2001	411	0.129	1.507	-0.095	-1.102	-0.051	-0.596
Total	6773	-0.330	-20.323	0.165	9.714**	0.081	4.740**

* Significant at the 5% level.
** Significant at the 1% level.

Table 2.6 presents the results for the pecking order preference by year during 1983-2001 for the LTD/TA measure. Again consistent with Claggett, Jr. (1992), all the years taken in our sample had positive and significant gamma values at the 0.01 percent level of significance. Furthermore, the pooled data showed that the gamma values were significant for all the years covered by our study at the 0.01 percent level of significance.

In our previous study (1999) of the optimality of capital structure against the Pecking Order Theory, we had used the *Fortune* magazine's list of the largest 500 companies in the U.S. manufacturing industries. Our sample was composed of 256 surviving firms, divided into twenty-one industries covering 1974-1992, but no surviving bias in the data was detected. Our main purpose here is to examine whether the results obtained

Table 2.5
Summary of Test for Pecking Order Preference
By Industry, 1983-2001

Industry	Obs.	Gamma	Z-test
Aerospace	290	0.593	8.875255**
Apparel	780	0.723	20.67572**
Beverage	123	0.642	6.574953**
Building Materials	117	0.604	5.795713**
Chemicals	258	0.684	10.63591**
Computers, Office Equip.	243	0.781	13.77979**
Electronics, Elec. Equip.	454	0.755	17.32723**
Food	345	0.530	8.217197**
Forest Products	389	0.579	9.913620**
Industrial & Farm Equip.	260	0.772	13.86212**
Metal Products	224	0.610	8.156889**
Metals	290	0.621	9.537569**
Mining, Crude oil Prod.	130	0.529	5.031159**
Motor Vehicles & Parts	356	0.738	14.57250**
Petroleum Refining	987	0.636	18.32556**
Pharmaceuticals	330	0.571	8.926712**
Publishing, Printing	458	0.671	13.67932**
Sci. & Photo Equip.	232	0.634	8.827903**
Soaps, Cosmetics	267	0.683	10.79606**
Textile	126	0.554	5.286185**
Tobacco	114	0.566	5.179273**
Total	6773	0.648	49.56342**

* Significant at the 5% level.
** Significant at the 1% level.

by the *COMPUSTAT* data file were corroborated by *Fortune*'s list of the largest 500 companies. The results are shown in tables 2.7 and 2.8.

Table 2.7 shows the value of gamma and the test-statistic (Z). We find that for the measure of LTD/TA, nineteen out of twenty-one industries had Z statistics which were significant either at the 1% or at the 5% level (two-tail test). For the measure of TD/TA, seventeen industries had significant Z statistics while for the measure of TE/TA, nineteen industries had significant Z statistics either at the 1% or at the 5% level (two-tail test). This proves that the overwhelming majority of firms had convergence toward the industry mean over a one-year interval. The pooled data also showed this tendency toward convergence when the Z statistics for all the three measures were significant at the 1% level.

Table 2.6
Summary of Test for Pecking Order Preference
By Year, 1983-2001

Year	Obs.	Gamma	Z-test
1983	297	0.728	12.95068**
1984	314	0.740	13.79375**
1985	318	0.700	12.34297**
1986	320	0.688	12.00360**
1987	321	0.762	14.92497**
1988	332	0.627	10.38265**
1989	334	0.654	11.16777**
1990	350	0.716	13.55721**
1991	352	0.570	9.213560**
1992	353	0.692	12.74742**
1993	360	0.614	10.42675**
1994	371	0.682	12.68721**
1995	379	0.744	15.33496**
1996	384	0.641	11.57363**
1997	384	0.703	13.69777**
1998	395	0.602	10.59079**
1999	398	0.703	13.93338**
2000	400	0.552	9.369940**
2001	411	0.669	12.90738**
Total	6773	0.648	49.56342**

* Significant at the 5% level.
** Significant at the 1% level.

Table 2.8 also shows this strong tendency toward convergence when the gamma values and Z statistics for all three measures were calculated for 1974-1992. Here, also, we find that the Z statistics for LTD/TA were positive and significant in fifteen out of nineteen one-year periods. For TD/TA, the Z statistics were significant in twelve out of nineteen years, while for TE/TA, they were significant in fifteen out of nineteen years, either at the 1% or 5% levels. Thus both tables 2.7 and 2.8 support the conclusions reached by Jalilvand and Harris (1984), Lev (1969), Marsh (1982), and Clagget, Jr. (1992), but not by BDH (1982), where they found no significant convergence over one-year intervals.

Concluding Remarks

We have thus seen from our empirical investigation of the optimal capital structure theory and the pecking order theory that both these

Table 2.7
Summary of Capital Structure Symmetric Convergence, By Industry 1974-1992
LTD/TA—Long-term debt over total assets; TD/TA—Total debt over total assets; TE/TA—Total equity over total assets.

		LTD/TA		TD/TA		TE/TA	
Industry	Obs.	Gamma	Z-Test	Gamma	Z-Test	Gamma	Z-Test
Aerospace	342	0.145	1.87615	0.355	4.34003**	0.372	4.5155939**
Apparel	990	0.493	3.01786**	0.122	0.85196	0.571	3.2981656**
Beverage	114	0.623	3.67936**	0.237	1.73840	0.245	1.7934062
Building Materials	120	0.317	2.32892*	0.193	1.46692	0.094	0.7249253
Chemicals	224	0.425	4.07151**	0.334	3.33186**	0.293	2.9648492**
Computers, Office Equip.	264	0.474	4.79539**	0.351	3.77625**	0.518	5.0908833**
Electronics, Elec. Equip.	385	0.351	4.56025**	0.374	4.81265**	0.431	5.3961697**
Food	350	0.432	5.15424**	0.42	5.04247**	0.441	5.2361553**
Forest Products	432	0.457	5.97433**	0.447	5.87689**	0.531	6.6132117**
Industrial & Farm Equip.	270	0.255	2.86499**	0.358	3.88404**	0.254	2.8545378**
Metal Products	246	0.401	4.07423**	0.251	2.69471**	0.302	3.1930794**
Metals	278	0.014	0.16504	0.415	4.45172**	0.355	3.9129317**
Mining, Crude	146	0.287	2.34906*	0.572	4.00887**	0.439	3.3701931**
Motor Vehicles	378	0.261	3.46392**	0.403	5.07071**	0.215	2.8867511**
Petroleum Refinery	1006	0.278	5.98935**	0.361	7.55070**	0.358	7.4972402**
Pharmaceuticals	299	0.521	5.43760**	0.482	5.16385**	0.572	5.7369596**
Publishing, Printing	554	0.386	5.92665**	0.426	6.41478**	0.467	6.8730964**
Sci. & Photo Eq.	242	0.396	4.00005**	0.373	3.80704**	0.352	3.6243339**
Soaps, Cosmetic	180	0.499	4.10259**	0.443	3.76792**	0.319	2.8683022**
Textile	138	0.064	0.53055	-0.036	-0.2988	0.179	1.4629284
Tobacco	97	0.347	2.26651	-0.035	-0.2436	0.388	2.4905201*
Total	6164	0.326	17.1101**	0.38	19.5142**	0.400	20.353212**

* Significant at the 5% level.
** Significant at the 1% level.

theories coexist, but the pecking order theory is more pronounced as all of the twenty-one industries had Z statistics that were statistically significant, while the optimal capital structure theory was statistically significant for nineteen out of the twenty-one industries. We have also found that firms will adjust their respective debt/ asset ratio toward the industry mean when it is above the mean, but the process of adjusting their capital structure toward the industry mean is slow when it is below the mean. Obviously, firms adjust their debt/ asset ratio more quickly if it is above the industry mean because of high cost of debt and the attendant default and market risks.

Table 2.8
Summary of Capital Structure Symmetric Convergence, By Year 1974-1992
LTD/TA—Long-term debt over total assets; TD/TA—Total debt over total assets; TE/TA—Total equity over total assets.

		LTD/TA		TD/TA		TE/TA	
Year	Obs.	Gamma	Z-Test	Gamma	Z-Test	Gamma	Z-Test
1974	287	0.365	4.07169**	0.352	3.94772**	0.357	3.995696**
1975	294	0.376	4.22180**	0.301	3.47818**	0.264	3.085497**
1976	294	0.363	4.10363**	0.309	3.56542**	0.464	4.986722**
1977	296	0.257	3.02069**	0.114	1.37744	0.128	1.543953
1978	297	0.265	3.11535**	0.101	1.22509	0.246	2.907053**
1979	299	0.358	4.09031**	0.145	1.75553	0.139	1.684358
1980	299	0.054	0.65980	0.183	2.20146*	0.178	2.143309*
1981	301	0.341	3.9321**	0.118	1.43728	-0.042	-0.51472
1982	305	0.097	1.19131	0.172	2.09080*	0.079	0.971792
1983	319	0.399	4.62090**	0.277	3.36164**	0.284	3.43926**
1984	328	0.149	1.88608	0.111	1.41215	0.208	2.604413**
1985	341	0.068	0.88559	0.097	1.26022	0.174	2.236678*
1986	342	0.901	5.10769**	0.022	0.28741	0.181	2.326147*
1987	357	0.343	4.30744**	0.317	4.01945**	0.375	4.647585**
1988	358	0.237	3.08134**	0.901	5.23092**	0.991	1.775314
1989	359	0.199	2.61253**	0.196	2.57474*	0.326	4.128603**
1990	363	0.077	1.03363	0.167	2.21687*	0.317	4.047891**
1991	363	0.178	2.35827*	0.061	0.81975	-0.014	-0.18847
1992	363	0.286	3.69210**	0.251	3.27326**	0.336	4.263486**
Total	6164	0.326	17.1100**	0.381	19.5568**	0.401	20.39431**

* Significant at the 5% level.
** Significant at the 1% level.

References

Bowen, R. M., L. A. Daley, and C. C. Huber, Jr., 1982, "Evidence on the Existence and Determinants of Inter-industry Differences in Leverage," *Financial Management*, Winter, 10-20.

Claggett, Jr., E. T., 1992, "Capital Structure: Convergent and Pecking Order Evidence," *Review of Financial Economics*, March, 35-48.

Donaldson, G, 1961, "Corporate Debt Capacity: A study of Corporate Debt Policy and the Determination of Corporate Debt Capacity," Boston: Division of Research, Harvard Graduate School of Business Administration.

Ghosh, Arvin and Francis Cai, 1999, "Capital Structure: New Evidence of Optimality and Pecking Order theory," *American Business Review*, 28, 32-38.

Goodman, L. A. and W. H. Kruskal, 1972, "Measures of Association for Cross-Classification, Part IV," *Journal of American Statistical Association*, 415-421; Part III, *Ibid*, 1963, 310-364; Part II, *Ibid*, 1959, 123-163; Part I, *Ibid*, 1954, 732-764.

Jalilvand, A., and R. S. Harris, 1984, "Corporate Behavior in Adjusting to Capital Structure and Dividend Targets: An Econometric Study," *Journal of Finance*, March, 127-145.

Lev, B., 1969, "Industry Averages as Targets for Financial Ratios," *Journal of Accounting Research*, Autumn, 290-299.

Marsh, P., 1982, "The Choice Between Equity and Debt: An Empirical Study," *The Journal of Finance*, March, 121-144.

Modigliani, F. and M. Miller, 1963, "Corporate Income Taxes and the Cost of Capital: A Correction," *American Economic Review*, 53, June, 433-443.

________, 1958, "The Cost of Capital, Corporation Finance, and the Theory of Investments," *American Economic Review*, 48, 261-297.

Myers, S. C., 1984, "The Capital Structure Puzzle," *The Journal of Finance*, July, 575-592.

Schwartz, E. and J. R. Aronson, 1967, "Some Surrogate Evidence in Support of the Concept of Optimal Financial Structure," *Journal of Finance*, March, 10-18.

Taggart, Jr., R. A., 1986, "Corporate Financing: Too Much Debt?" *Financial Analysts Journal*, May-June, 35-42.

3

Tests of Capital Structure Theory: A Binomial Approach

Despite "Optimal Capital Structure Theory" and "Pecking Order Theory" having long been recognized as two important developments in the capital structure theory, financial academics and practitioners still have little agreement on what determines the capital structure of a firm and what theory a firm will follow in formulating its mix of the debt and equity. In this chapter we draw on recent progress in the theory of capital structure to analyze empirically these two theories that exist in the academic finance world and that have drawn a great deal of debate ever since they were developed.

The article published by Miller and Modigliani (MM) (1958) contains the argument that a firm's capital structure is irrelevant with regard to its value under the assumption of perfect markets and no transaction costs. In their subsequent article (1963), MM showed the impact of corporate income taxes on the capital structure of a firm and found that a firm will increase the use of debt to take advantage of the tax deductibility of interest, but there exists a market equilibrium in which the benefit of using debt financing is equal to the increased bankruptcy costs due to the firm's high leverage. This finding and subsequent researches by Miller (1977) and DeAngelo/Masulis (1980) led to the theory of "Optimal Capital structure," the debt and equity mix where the firm's value is maximized.

Donaldson (1961) found "management strongly favored internal generation as a source of new funds even to the exclusion of external funds." Stewart C. Myers published an article in 1984 which characterizes Donaldson's view of the firm's financing decision in what he termed "Pecking Order Theory." Pecking-order theory states that "the firms in general prefer internal financing (first), then external debt-financing (second), and external equity-financing (third)."

In this chapter, we continue the investigation whether a firm's Debt/Equity mix follows "optimal capital structure" theory or "pecking order" theory. We use the criteria of the industry mean as a predicator of a firm's capital structure as in Claggett Jr. (1992) and Ghosh and Cai (1999). A binomial model is constructed and is used to perform the empirical test on the financial data of the 2001 Fortune 500 manufacturing companies. The result of our paper shows that the probability that a firm's debt level is moving toward the industry's mean is not significantly different from the probability that it is moving further away from the industry mean. But the probability that a firm's debt level is moving toward the industry's mean is very high when it is above the industry mean. This empirical result suggests that the optimal capital structure is not a single point, rather it is a range of values from zero to the industry mean within which a typical U.S. firm will be indifferent to the firm's debt level. In other words, a firm will only adjust the capital structure when the firm's debt level is out of this range. The second result of this paper generally agrees with pecking order theory. That is, firms prefer using internal financing as opposed to using external financing. Furthermore, when external funds are required, a firm prefers debt financing to equity financing.

Hypothesis and Proposition

In this section, we develop three hypotheses and three lemmas. Let V be the value of a firm and L be the debt level of the firm's capital structure. Following the classification of industry mean as the optimal capital structure (Schwartz and Aronson(1967), Claggett, Jr. (1992)), we have the following hypothesis:

Hypothesis I. If there exists an optimal capital structure L^*, then a firm's value is maximized at L^*, $V_t^*=f(L_t^*)$ with $V_t/L_t < 0$ if $L>L^*$ and $V_t/L_t > 0$ if $L<L^*$.

Explanation of Hypothesis I: By definition, the optimal capital structure is the point where the firm's value is maximized. Under the assumption that the goal of the firm is to maximize the value of the firm, if a firm's capital structure is away from the optimal capital structure, then the firm will try to "correct" it (see Claggett, Jr. (1992)). That is, when a firm's capital structure is below the $\mathbf{L}^*$, the firm will adjust its capital structure upward, and when a firm's capital structure is above $\mathbf{L}^*$, the firm will adjust its capital structure downward. To test the hypothesis I we have developed Lemma I as follows:

Lemma I a. Suppose there are n periods and let N be the number of times a firm adjusted its capital structure toward the optimal capital structure; M be the number of times a firm's capital structure moved away from the optimal capital structure during n periods. If hypothesis I is true, then p = (N/n) will be significantly greater than ½ or 1-p = (M/n) will be significantly smaller than ½.

Lemma I is the extension of Hypothesis I, or simply another form of Hypothesis I. If Hypothesis I is valid, then we should observe higher number N than M. That is, if Hypothesis I is true, a firm will adjust its capital structure toward the optimal point to maximize the firm's value. Therefore, N is greater than M. If N is not statistically greater than M, then we reject Hypothesis I.

Hypothesis Ib. If there exists an optimal capital structure range R^*, then a firm's value is maximized for $L\ R^*$, $V_t^*=f(L_t\ \ R^*)>V_t^*=f(L_t\ \ R^*)$.

Explanation of Hypothesis Ib: By definition, the optimal capital structure range is a range of points where the firm's value is maximized. Under the assumption that the goal of the firm is to maximize the value of the firm, if a firm's capital structure is away from the optimal capital structure range, then the firm will try to "correct" it (see Claggett, Jr. (1992)).

Lemma I b. Suppose there are n periods and let N be the number of times a firm adjusted its capital structure toward the optimal capital structure range and M be the number of times a firm's capital structure moved away from the optimal capital structure range during n periods. When hypothesis Ib is true, then p =(N/M+N) will be significantly greater than ½ for the firms whose capital structure is out of the range R.

Lemma Ib is the extension of Hypothesis Ib. If Hypothesis Ib is valid, then we should observe higher number N than M when the firm's debt level is out of the optimal range. That is, if Hypothesis Ib is true, a firm will adjust its capital structure toward the optimal range to maximize the firm's value when its debt level is not in that range. Therefore, we should observe greater N than M for the firms whose debt level is not in the range.

Hypothesis II. Firms generally prefer internal financing to external financing.

To test Hypothesis II, we construct another form of Hypothesis II. We call it Lemma II as follows:

Lemma II. Suppose there are n periods and let P be the number of times a firm used internal financing and Q be the number of times a firm used external financing. If hypothesis II is true, then p(P/P+Q) will be significantly greater than 1/2.

To see what form of external funds is preferred when a firm needs outside funds, we constructed the following hypothesis:

Hypothesis III. When a firm needs external funds, it generally prefers a safer security (Debt) to a less safer security (Equity).

We constructed Lemma III to test Hypothesis III:

Lemma III. Suppose there are n periods and let S be the number of times a firm used debt financing and T be the number of times a firm used equity financing. If hypothesis III is true, then p (S/S+T) will be significantly greater than 1/2.

Hypothesis I and Lemma I are used to test the optimal capital structure theory, while Hypotheses II, Lemma II, Hypothesis III, and Lemma III are for the testing of pecking order theory.

Sample Data and Test Model

A. Sample Data

The sample data are selected from the 2001 Fortune 500 largest manufacturing companies. The sample used for analysis contains firms that are in industries other than finance, insurance, and real estate, and that have no accounting changes and/or data errors. The sample covers years from 1982 to 2001 and twenty-one industries.

Following Claggett Jr. (1992), a firm is said to follow the optimal capital structure theory in year t if the firm adjusts its long term debt ratio toward the industry mean. $MOVEMN_t$ is defined as the indicator variable of whether a firm follows the optimal capital structure theory or not,

$$MOVEMN_t = \begin{cases} 1, & \text{if the capital structure is moving toward the industry mean in year t} \\ 0, & \text{otherwise.} \end{cases}$$

INT_t is defined as the indicator variable of whether a firm uses internal funds or not,

$$INT_t = \begin{cases} 1, & \text{if a firm uses internal funds in year t} \\ 0, & \text{otherwise.} \end{cases}$$

$DEBT_t$ is defined as the indicator variable of whether a firm uses debt or not in a given year when it uses external financing,

$$DEBT_t = \begin{cases} 1, & \text{if a firm uses debt when external funds are required in a given year t} \\ 0, & \text{otherwise.} \end{cases}$$

Let $LTDRATIO_t$ be the variable of debt ratio in time t and $LTDMN_t$ the industry mean in time t respectively. D_t is defined as the difference of $LTDRATIO_t$ and $LTDMN_t$ ($D_t = LTDRATIO_t - LTDMN_t$). $ADJUST_t$ is defined as an indicator of variable of whether a firm follows the optimal capital structure theory or not ($ADJUST_t = LTDRATIO_t - LTDRATIO_{t-1}$).

Table 3.1 through Table 3.3 provide a brief statistical description of the data. Table 3.1 shows that the unconditional probabilities that firms' capital structure will move toward the industry mean are close to 50 percent across the industries and the similar results year by year. Table 3.1 shows that a firm's capital structure movement exhibits the characteristic of random walk, which has no predictable pattern and is contradictory to optimal capital structure theory. Table 3.2 gives the statistics whether a firm uses internal financing or external financing industry by industry and year by year respectively. The percentage of firms using internal financing is significantly higher than 50 percent except for three industries: computer and office equipment, industrial and farm equipment, and mining and crude oil. Table 3.3 strongly supports the notion that when the external financing is required, firms prefer using debt than equity.

To proceed with our analysis, we use the following sampling method to build two working data: sample one—to analyze whether a firm follows the optimal capital structure theory in a given industry, we pool the data of the companies in that industry from 1982 to 2001, recording a firm nineteen times in the sample; sample two—to analyze whether a firm follows the optimal capital structure theory in a given year, we pool the data of all the companies in that year, recording a firm once in the sample. Sample one is also used in analyzing whether firms follow internal financing or external financing in a given industry and sample two is also used in analyzing whether firms follow external or internal financing in a given year.

Table 3.1
The Likelihood of Moving Toward the Industry Mean by Industry and by Year
The likelihood of moving toward the industry mean is defined as the expected value of MOVEMN, E(MOVEMN), where MOVEMN=1 if a firm's capital structure moves toward the industry mean in a given year and MOVEMN=0 otherwise. N is the sample size.

Industry	E(MOVEMN)	N	Year	E(MOVEMN)	N
Aerospace	48.98	290	1983	52.47	297
Apparel	54.59	780	1984	55.11	314
Beverage	50.79	123	1985	50.89	318
Building Materials	52.47	117	1986	51.46	320
Chemicals	46.66	258	1987	49.31	321
Computers, Office Equip.	55.15	243	1988	49.30	332
Electronics, Elec. Equip.	51.82	454	1989	49.60	334
Food	49.12	345	1990	52.41	350
Forest Products	57.46	389	1991	55.13	352
Industrial & Farm Equip.	50.14	260	1992	53.12	353
Metal Products	51.22	224	1993	49.89	360
Metals	47.24	290	1994	53.23	371
Mining, Crude oil Prod.	55.79	130	1995	55.67	379
Motor Vehicles & Parts	53.36	356	1996	53.93	384
Petroleum Refining	52.82	987	1997	54.67	384
Pharmaceuticals	57.87	330	1998	53.76	395
Publishing, Printing	55.75	458	1999	49.06	398
Sci. & Photo Equip.	54.53	232	2000	54.37	400
Soaps, Cosmetics	56.45	267	2001	48.32	411
Textile	47.66	126	Total	52.37	6773
Tobacco	49.98	114			
Total	52.37	6773			

Table 3.2
The Likelihood of Using Internal Financing
by Industry and by Year
The likelihood of using internal funds is defined as the expected value of INT, where INT=1 if a firm uses internal funds in a given year and INT=0 otherwise. N is the sample size. E(INT) is expressed in percentage.

Industry	E(INT)	N	Year	E(INT)	N
Aerospace	70.5	252	1983	70.1	258
Apparel	68.2	663	1984	72.0	264
Beverage	68.2	102	1985	80.1	270
Building Materials	79.0	102	1986	80.3	280
Chemicals	68.7	240	1987	80.6	287
Computers, Office Equip.	57.6	199	1988	77.1	290
Electronics, Elec. Equip.	72.1	395	1989	71.4	292
Food	70.2	286	1990	70.7	297
Forest Products	65.7	340	1991	76.9	302
Industrial & Farm Equip.	54.0	235	1992	81.1	307
Metal Products	68.4	193	1993	82.8	310
Metals	67.2	244	1994	65.5	312
Mining, Crude oil Prod.	58.0	114	1995	52.7	325
Motor Vehicles & Parts	62.7	312	1996	58.7	336
Petroleum Refining	69.8	869	1997	65.4	339
Pharmaceuticals	78.8	289	1998	55.1	346
Publishing, Printing	71.1	403	1999	59.3	350
Sci. & Photo Equip.	68.1	203	2000	56.8	352
Soaps, Cosmetics	69.7	236	2001	58.1	360
Textile	64.8	105			
Tobacco	68.5	95			
Total	68.2	5877		68.2	5877

Table 3.3
The Likelihood a Firm uses Debt when the firm Needs External Financing by Industry and by year
The likelihood of using internal funds is defined as the expected value of DEBT,E($DEBT_t$), where DEBT=1 if a firm uses debt financing in a given year t and DEBT=0 otherwise.

Industry	E(D)	N	Year	E(D)	N
AEROSPACE	91.6	95	1974	97.5	79
APPAREL	85.7	21	1975	92.4	92
BEVERAGE	94.1	34	1976	84.2	57
BUILDING MATERIALS	96.9	32	1977	97.9	47
CHEMICAL	96.2	52	1978	92.7	55
COMPUTER,OFF.EQUIP.	75.	92	1979	90	60
ELECTRONICS,ELEC.	77.9	104	1980	84.6	78
FOOD	94.6	93	1981	87	77
FOREST PRO.	90.9	121	1982	84.9	73
INDUSTRIAL and FARM EQUIP	92.4	79	1983	61.8	55
METAL PRODUCTS	85.4	82	1984	90.9	55
METALS	94.3	70	1985	93.3	90
MINING, CRUDE OIL PRO.	83.1	59	1986	85	113
MOTOR VEHICLE AND PART	93.3	89	1987	82.5	103
PETROLEUM REFINING	90.4	239	1988	92.2	115
PHARMACEUTICALS	84.6	52	1989	88.1	143
PUBLISHING,PRINTING	92.1	178	1990	94.4	124
SCIENCE AND PHOTO EQUIP	85.3	68	1991	90.3	134
SOAPS, COSMETICS	82.6	46	1992	90.8	119
TEXTILE	91.1	45			
TOBACCO	83.3	18			
Average	88.9			88.9	
TOTAL	1669			1669	

B. Test Method

To test Lemma I, we use Z-test on the binomial variable MOVEMN. We use Z-test on binomial variable INT for Lemma II, and for Lemma III, Z-test is used on the binomial variable DEBT.

The test procedure of this paper can be summarized as follows: first we look at the binomial variable MOVEMN to see whether a firm's capital structure moves toward the mean or not; then we look the binomial variable INT to see whether a firm prefers internal financing or not; finally, we look at the binomial variable DEBT to test whether firms prefer debt or equity when external funds are needed.

Empirical Results

This section presents the empirical results for tests on Hypothesis I, Lemma I, Lemma II, and Lemma III.

A. Test on Lemma Ia

Table 3.4 presents the Z-test results on Lemma I. With the exception of the industries pharmaceuticals and soaps, cosmetics, the Z-scores are not significant. This suggests that p (N/(N+M)) is not significantly greater than 50 percent. There is no convergence towards the means. Thus, we reject the hypothesis that a firm will adjust its capital structure towards the industry mean.

B. Test on Lemma Ib

In Table 3.5, we presented the test results for Lemma Ib. All the z-scores are significant for every industry and for every year. This suggests that p (N/(N+M)) is significantly greater than 50 percent. When a firm's debt level is out of the range, it will try to correct it and converge back to the range. Why does a firm adjust the capital structure toward the industry mean when it is above the mean, while it is indifferent when the capital structure is below the mean? The possible explanation for this is as follows: when a firm's debt level reaches a significantly high level, the high cost of the debt associated with the high leverage makes the reduction of the debt a meaningful task. That's why we observe more firms adjusting their debt level downward while the firms which have below average debt level do not put the consideration of debt level as their first priority. Some other factors, such as the availability of the funds, might play a more important role in the consideration of the firm's capital structure.

Table 3.4
Results of Z-test on Lemma Ia
by Industry and by Year
Null hypothesis H_0: p>=½, where p=N/(N+M)

Industry	Z-test	Year	Z-test
AEROSPACE	-0.9928	1975	0.35675
APPAREL	1.069415	1976	0.4080
BEVERAGE	0.278819	1977	-0.409409
BUILDING MATERIALS	0.689348	1978	-0.58099
CHEMICAL	-1.33268	1979	-0.24005
COMPUTER, OFF. EQUIP.	1.483455	1980	-0.17176
ELECTRONICS, ELEC. EQU	-0.50147	1981	0.758282
FOOD	0.614827	1982	1.659995
FOREST PRO.	1.386818	1983	0.935307
INDUSTRIAL , FARM EQUIP	-0.90723	1984	-0.21332
METAL PRODUCTS	0.858464	1985	0.940323
METALS	-0.39942	1986	1.799041
MINING, CRUDE OIL PRO.	1.108244	1987	2.071243
MOTOR VEHICLE AND PART	1.182929	1988	1.380452
PETROLEUM REFINING	0.177989	1989	2.244994
PHARMACEUTICALS	2.322272	1990	-0.74833
PUBLISHING, PRINTING	1.106085	1991	1.159914
SCIENCE AND PHOTO EQUIP	2.244531	1992	-1.08508
SOAPS, COSMETICS	2.177		
TEXTILE	0.172604		
TOBACCO	0.142829		

Table 3.5
Results of Z-test on Lemma Ib
by Industry and by Year
Null hypothesis H_0: >=½, where p=N/(N+M)

Industry	Z-test	Year	Z-test
AEROSPACE	8.6386767		
APPAREL	2.8867467		
BEVERAGE	5.4221767	1974	9.6847372
BUILDING MATERIALS	4.5254834	1975	7.9056942
CHEMICAL	8.1010489	1976	8.8244068
COMPUTER, OFF. EQUIP.	4.8585004	1977	9.0519556
ELECTRONICS, ELEC. EQU	8.168422	1978	9.0756195
FOOD	8.2731575	1979	7.8360076
FOREST PRO.	10.203639	1980	9.2063341
INDUSTRIAL , FARM EQUI	6.2629551	1981	8.7197762
METAL PRODUCTS	6.464984	1982	8.1115513
METALS	7.3703012	1983	7.4855489
MINING, CRUDE OIL PRO.	4.2759301	1984	7.0235843
MOTOR VEHICLE AND PART	10.293356	1985	5.6664257
PETROLEUM REFINING	14.220763	1986	11.7047
PHARMACEUTICALS	7.1203932	1987	2.8167581
PUBLISHING, PRINTING	9.7612996	1988	7.4409732
SCIENCE AND PHOTO EQUI	6.6	1989	6.4100645
SOAPS, COSMETICS	6.6856298	1990	9.6242671
TEXTILE	4.6615651	1991	9.2641359
TOBACCO	2.0816702		
TOTAL	36.07947	TOTAL	36.07947

C. Test on Lemma II

The test results on Lemma II are provided in table 3.6. From table 3.6, we see that only industries Mining, Crude Oil Products, Industrial, Farm Equipment do not provide significant results. At 2.5 percent level, the rest of the industries indicate Hypothesis II is true. That is, a typical U.S. firm prefers internal financing to external financing.

D. Test on Lemma III

According to Hypothesis III, when a firm needs outside funds, it prefers debt over equity. We constructed Lemma III to test the validity of Hypothesis III. Table 3.7 contains the test results. The results provide strong evidence for the hypothesis that a firm prefers debt financing. All Z-test values are significant at 2.5 percent level in every industry and every year except 1983.

Concluding Remarks

In this chapter, we have analyzed further whether a firm's capital structure follows the optimal capital structure theory or the pecking order theory. Following the industry mean as a predicator of a firm's capital structure, we have constructed three hypotheses and have used a binomial model to perform the empirical tests on the financial data of *Fortune 500* manufacturing companies. The first finding of this chapter shows that, in general, the probability that a firm's debt level is moving toward the industry mean is not significantly different from the probability that it is moving further away from the industry mean, while the probability that a firm's debt level is moving toward the industry's mean is very high when it is above the industry mean. This empirical result suggests that the optimal capital structure is not a single point; rather it is a range of values from zero to the industry mean within which a typical U.S. firm will be indifferent to the firm's debt level. In other words, a firm will only adjust to the optimal capital structure when the firm's debt level is out of this range. The second result of this chapter generally agrees with the pecking order theory, that is, firms prefer using internal financing as opposed to using external financing. Third, when external funds are required, a firm prefers debt financing to equity financing.

Table 3.6
Results Z-test on Lemma II
by Industry and by Year
Null hypothesis H_0: p<=½, where p=P/(P+Q)

Industry	Z-Test	Year	Z-test
AEROSPACE	5.742719	1974	6.171661
APPAREL	2.672	1975	4.847079
BEVERAGE	3.656333	1976	8.587916
BUILDING MATERIALS	4.988306	1977	10.18386
CHEMICAL	4.247881	1978	8.735473
COMPUTER, OFF. EQUIP.	2.414904	1979	8.444072
ELECTRONICS, ELEC. EQU	7.006083	1980	6.377376
FOOD	6.688	1981	6.465903
FOREST PRO.	5.343545	1982	6.866573
INDUSTRIAL , FARM EQUIP	1.064911	1983	8.207289
METAL PRODUCTS	3.937598	1984	8.608862
METALS	3.556011	1985	4.115551
MINING, CRUDE OIL PRO.	0.778763	1986	1.163386
MOTOR VEHICLE AND PART	2.891055	1987	2.834929
PETROLEUM REFINING	11.66622	1988	3.269172
PHARMACEUTICALS	9.140244	1989	1.099818
PUBLISHING, PRINTING	6.573265	1990	3.24758
SCIENCE AND PHOTO EQUIP	4.39377	1991	2.279649
SOAPS, COSMETICS	4.857655	1992	2.279649
TEXTILE	3.392481		
TOBACCO	2.298159		
TOTAL	22.70878	TOTAL	22.70878

Table 3.7
Results of Z-test on Lemma III
by Industry and by Year
Null hypothesis H_0: p<=½, where p=S/(S+T)

Industry	Z-value	Year	Z-value
AEROSPACE	8.109333	1974	8.443785
APPAREL	3.271959	1975	8.13373
BEVERAGE	5.1429	1976	5.164087
BUILDING MATERIALS	5.306129	1977	6.567717
CHEMICAL	6.663059	1978	6.333434
COMPUTER, OFF. EQUIP.	4.795832	1979	6.196773
ELECTRONICS, ELEC. EQU	5.690506	1980	6.111579
FOOD	8.602136	1981	6.493474
FOREST PRO.	8.998	1982	5.963715
INDUSTRIAL, FARM EQUIP	7.537189	1983	1.750223
METAL PRODUCTS	6.411213	1984	6.06645
METALS	7.412808	1985	8.215597
MINING, CRUDE OIL PRO.	5.084918	1986	7.441102
MOTOR VEHICLE AND PART	8.169828	1987	6.59678
PETROLEUM REFINING	12.49138	1988	9.050892
PHARMACEUTICALS	4.990083	1989	9.112195
PUBLISHING,PRINTING	11.23368	1990	9.88835
SCIENCE AND PHOTO EQUIP	5.821825	1991	9.330125
SOAPS, COSMETICS	4.422079	1992	8.901509
TEXTILE	5.514144		
TOBACCO	2.825599		
TOTAL	31.78394	TOTAL	31.78394

References

Bowen, R. M., L. A. Daley, and C. C. Huber, Jr., 1982, "Evidence on the Existence and Determinants of Inter-Industry Differences in Leverage," *Financial Management*, Winter, 10-20.

Claggett, Jr., E.T., 1992, "Capital Structure: Convergent and Pecking Order Evidence," *Review of Financial Economics*, March, 35-48.

DeAngelo, H. and R.W. Masulis, 1980, "Optimal Capital Structure under Corporate and Personal Taxation," *Journal of Financial Economics* 8, 3-30.

Donaldson, G, 1961, "Corporate Debt Capacity: A Study of Corporate Debt Policy and the Determination of Corporate Debt Capacity," Boston: Division of Research, Harvard Graduate School of Business Administration.

Ghosh, Arvin and Francis Cai, 1999, "Capital structure: new evidence of optimality and Pecking Order theory," *American Business Review*, Volume 28, No 1, January, page 32-38.

Goodman, L. A. and W. H. Kruskal, "Measures of Association for Cross-Classification, Part IV," *Journal of American Statistical Association*, 1972, 415-421; Part III, *Ibid*, 1963, 310-364; Part II, *Ibid*, 1959, 123-163; Part I, *Ibid*, 1954, 732-764.

Jalilvand, A. and R. S. Harris, 1984, "Corporate Behavior in Adjusting to Capital Structure and Dividend Targets: An Econometric Study," *Journal of Finance*, March, 127-145.

Lev, B., 1969, "Industry Averages as Targets for Financial Ratios," *Journal of Accounting Research*, Autumn, 290-299.

Marsh, P., 1982, "The Choice Between Equity and Debt: An Empirical Study," *The Journal of Finance*, March, 121-144.

Miller, M. 1997, "Death and Taxes," *Journal of Finance* 32, 261-276.

Modigliani, F. and M. Miller, 1963, "Corporate Income Taxes and the Cost of Capital: A Correction," *American Economic Review* 53, June, 433-443.

________, 1958, "The Cost of Capital, Corporation Finance, and the Theory of Investments," *American Economic Review* 48, 261-297.

Myers, S. C., 1984, "The Capital Structure Puzzle," *The Journal of Finance*, July, 575-592.

Schwartz, E. and J. R. Aronson, 1967, "Some Surrogate Evidence in Support of the Concept of Optimal Financial Structure," *Journal of Finance*, March, 10-18.

Taggart, Jr., R. A., 1986, "Corporate Financing: Too Much Debt?" *Financial Analysts Journal*, May/June, 35-42.

4

The Determinants of Capital Structure

Introduction

Rajan and Zingales (1995) use four key independent variables to analyze the determinants of capital structure: asset structure, growth opportunities, firm size, and profitability. They find that leverage increases with asset structure and size, but decreases with growth opportunities and profitability. However, in an earlier article (1991), Kale, Noe, and Ramirez took non-debt tax shields, firm size, and business risk (i.e., volatility of cash flows) as the cross-sectional determinants of capital structure and had found that non-debt tax shields and firm size had positive signs, but business risk was decreasing first and then increasing with the optimal debt level.

In this chapter, we choose nine variables to test the determinants of capital structure: asset size, growth of assets, non-debt tax shields, fixed asset ratio, profit margin, research and development expenditure, advertising expenditure, selling expenses, and the coefficient of variation of cash flows as business risk (volatility). We have also run the tests with and without business risk to see the change of signs and robustness of the test results. Further, we have used the dummy variables for industry classification to see whether industry characteristics have any impact on the capital structure.

Data Source and Methodology

The data used in this study are from *COMPUSTAT Research Insights* 2003. Our sample is composed of 411 firms, divided into nineteen industries. We have selected two years—1992 and 2002—for our cross-sectional studies. To analyze the determinants of capital structure, we use the ordinary least square (OLS) equations, with the long-term debt ratio (Long-Term Debt/ Total Assets) as the dependent variable, and asset size, growth of assets, non-debt tax shields (depreciation allowance and investment tax credit), fixed assets to total assets ratio, net profit margin, research and development expenditure (%), advertising expenditure (%), and selling expenses (%) as independent variables.

In order to test the relationship between capital structure and its determinants, we estimate the following multiple regression equation for our sample:

$$Y=\beta_0+\beta_1 AS+\beta_2 GA+\beta_3 NDTS+\beta_4 RFATA+\beta_5 NPM+\beta_6 RD+\beta_7 ADV + \beta_8 SE+\varepsilon$$

where

Y= Long Term Debt / Total Assets;
AS= Asset Size;
GA= Growth of Assets;
NDTS= Non-Debt Tax Shield;
FATA= Fixed Assets/Total Assets;
NPM= Net Profit Margin;
RD= Research and Development Expenditure (%);
ADV= Advertising Expenditure (%);
SE= Selling Expense (%);
CV= Coefficient of Variation of Cash Flows.

To see how business risk affects leverage, we add the volatility of cash flows in the regression equation. We use coefficient of variation of cash flows as a proxy for the business risk and assume the leverage has a quadratic relationship with COCF. The equation is now:

$$Y=\beta_0+\beta_1 AS+\beta_2 GA+\beta_3 NDTS+\beta_4 RFATA+\beta_5 NPM+\beta_6 RD+\beta_7 ADV + \beta_8 SE+\beta_9 CVCF+\beta_{10} CVCF^2+\varepsilon$$

Kale, Noe and Ramirez (1988) use the industry dummy variables in their paper. To see if industry characteristics play a role in the determinants of capital structure, we include the industry dummies as explanatory variables in our analysis. The equation becomes:

$$Y=\beta_0+\beta_1 AS+\beta_2 GA+\beta_3 NDTS+\beta_4 RFATA+\beta_5 NPM+\beta_6 RD+\beta_7 ADV + \beta_8 SE+\beta_9 CVCF+\beta_{10} CVCF^2+\beta_{D1} D_1+\beta_{D2} D_2+\ldots+\beta_{D18} D_{18}+\varepsilon$$

where $\beta_{D1,}$ β_{D2}... β_{D18} are the coefficients for industry dummy variables D_1 through D_{18}.

Following the traditional capital structure theory, we would expect the signs of β_1, β_3, and β_4 to be positive, and the signs of β_2, β_5, β_6, β_7, and β_8 to be negative. As for β_9 and β_{10}, the relationship is expected to be first positive and then negative, according to the traditional capital structure theory. The results are shown in tables 4.1 through 4.6.

The Results

In table 4.1, we have shown the regression results for the year 2002. We find that the growth of assets, fixed asset ratio, and the R & D expenditure (%) are significant at the 1 percent level, while profit margin is significant at the 12 percent level.

The negative sign of the β-coefficient for the growth of assets conforms to the conclusion reached by Smith and Watts (1992). Smith and Watts (1992) provide the empirical evidence that support the negative relationship between leverage and growth opportunities. Myers and Majluf (1984), Harris and Raviv (1991), Smith and Watts (1992), and

Table 4.1
Capital Structure Determinants—Year 2002
(Long-Term Debt Ratio as Dependent Variable)

$$Y=\beta_0 + \beta_1 AS + \beta_2 GA + \beta_3 NDTS + \beta_4 RFATA + \beta_5 NPM + \beta_6 RD + \beta_7 ADV + \beta_8 SE + \varepsilon$$

Independent Variable	Coefficient	t-Value
Total Assets	0.00004	0.31450
Growth Of Assets	-0.21600	-3.44538**
Depreciation	0.00225	0.62109
Investment Tax Credit	0.02436	0.28634**
Fixed Asset Ratio	0.10146	3.47803
Profit Margin	-0.11393	-1.59622*
R&D Expenditure (%)	-0.78970	-2.41570**
Ad. Expenditure (%)	0.05835	0.15621
Selling Expenditure (%)	0.00168	0.01950

* Significant at the 12% level
** Significant at the 1% level
Data source: *COMPUSTAT Research Insights* 2003

Rajan and Zingales (1995) find that firms expecting high future growth use a greater amount of equity finance. Their results show that there is a negative relationship between profitability and leverage. In our result, the coefficient of profitability has a negative sign and it is significant at the 12 percent level. As for the fixed asset ratio (fixed assets/ total assets), its contribution is very small, although the positive sign means the increase of fixed assets has a collateral value for higher debt. But the negative sign of the β-coefficient for R & D expenditure indicates that firm leverage increases with the decrease in R & D expenditure, again confirming the conclusion reached by Harris and Raviv (1991).

Table 4.2 presents the regression results for the year 1992. The overall importance and signs on the β-coefficients for growth of assets, investment tax credit, fixed asset ratio, research & development expenditure, advertising expenditure (%), and selling expenditure are similar to those reported in year 2002, except that the depreciation has a negative sign, and the profitability doesn't have a robust significance.

In tables 4.3 and 4.4 we present the results of capital structure determinants with business risk. We estimate the business risk as the coefficient

Table 4.2
Capital Structure Determinants—Year 1992
(Long Term Debt Ratio as Dependent Variable)

$$Y=\beta_0 + \beta_1 AS + \beta_2 GA + \beta_3 NDTS + \beta_4 RFATA + \beta_5 NPM + \beta_6 RD + \beta_7 ADV + \beta_8 SE + \varepsilon$$

Independent Variable	Coefficient	t-Value
Asset	0.0000492	0.370000
Growth of Assets	-0.1979850	-3.158000**
Depreciation	-0.0021442	-0.591000
Investment Tax Credit	0.0308000	0.362000
Fixed Asset Ratio	0.0811000	2.780000**
Profit Margin	-0.0808000	-1.042000
R&D Expenditure (%)	-0.8678000	-2.842000**
Ad. Expenditure (%)	0.0452000	0.121000
Selling Expenditure (%)	-0.0012929	-0.015000

* --Significance at 12% level
**--Significance at 1% level
Data source: *COMPUSTAT Research Insights* 2003

Table 4.3
Capital Structure Determinants—Year 2002
(Long-Term Debt Ratio as Dependent Variable)

$$Y=\beta_0 + \beta_1 AS + \beta_2 GA + \beta_3 NDTS + \beta_4 RFATA + \beta_5 NPM + \beta_6 RD + \beta_7 ADV + \beta_8 SE + \beta_9 CVCF + \beta_{10} CVCF^2 + \varepsilon$$

Independent Variable	Coefficient	t-Value
COCF1	23.123	0.7565
COCF2	-7.8296	-1.6905*
Asset	0.0000	0.2219
Growth of Assets	-26.917	-4.291**
Depreciation	0.0011	0.3060
Investment Tax Credit	-0.0142	-0.1655
Fixed Asset Ratio	0.0763	2.5781**
Profit Margin	0.0376	0.4820
R&D Expenditure (%)	-0.7397	-2.4234**
Ad. Expenditure (%)	-0.0242	-0.0649
Selling Expenditure (%)	0.0244	0.2905

* --Significant at the 12% level
**--Significant at the 1% level
Data source: *COMPUSTAT Research Insights* 2003

Table 4.4
Capital Structure Determinants—Year 1992
(Long Term Debt Ratio as Dependent Variable)

$$Y=\beta_0 + \beta_1 AS + \beta_2 GA + \beta_3 NDTS + \beta_4 RFATA + \beta_5 NPM + \beta_6 RD + \beta_7 ADV + \beta_8 SE + \beta_9 CVCF + \beta_{10} CVCF^2 + \varepsilon$$

Independent Variable	Coefficient	t-Value
COCF1	27.206	0.8900
COCF2	-4.3021	-0.819
Asset	0.0000	0.2610
Growth of Assets	-19.227	-3.065**
Depreciation	-0.0013	-0.3610
Investment Tax Credit	0.0129	0.1500
Fixed Asset Ratio	0.0898	3.033**
Profit Margin	-0.0940	-1.2050
R&D Expenditure (%)	-0.8702	-2.851**
Ad. Expenditure (%)	0.0384	0.1030
Selling Expenditure (%)	-0.0132	-0.1570

* --Significant at the 12% level
**--Significant at the 1% level
Data source: *COMPUSTAT Research Insights* 2003

of variation of cash flows (COCF) over the available time period. For the year 2002, the β-coefficient for COCF1 is not significant at either the 10 percent or the 1 percent level, while COCF2 has a significant coefficient at the 10 percent level. For the year 1992, β-coefficients for COCF1 and COCF2 are not significant in table 4.4. Whereas Kale, Noe, and Ramirez (1988) found the relationship between business risk and leverage to be quadratic—first decreasing and then increasing, we have found it to be the opposite—first increasing and then decreasing. Our result conforms to the traditional capital structure theory which suggests that when risk is low, firms will increase the debt level, but with higher risk, debt level would be lower.

Tables 4.5 and 4.6 show the β-coefficients of the nine capital structure determinants with risk and industry dummy variables for 1992 and 2002. Here, again, the growth of assets, fixed asset ratio, and R & D expenditure were significant at the 1 percent level in table 4.5. But the growth of assets variable was not significant in table 4.6. Similarly, advertising expenditure variable was not significant in table 4.5 but was significant at the 1 percent level in table 4.6.

When we include the dummy variables as proxy for industry characteristics, as done in tables 4.5 and 4.6, we have found that only industries 1 and 2 had positive signs for 1992 and 2002, respectively, while 8 and 6 have negative signs for the two selected years, respectively. Our results thus conform to that of Kale, Noe and Ramirez (1988) in this regard. In their paper, Kale, Noe and Ramirez (1988) find only three industry dummies having positive signs, while twelve had negative signs.

Concluding Remarks

Our results thus confirm the usefulness of taking growth of assets, fixed asset ratio, and R & D expenditure as the determinants of capital structure. At the same time, our results show that the relationship between business risk and leverage is quadratic, and it is first increasing and then decreasing—a relationship closer to the traditional theory. But the problem of omitted variables remains as the known determinants "explain" a very small percentage of the variation in capital structure. All this indicates that nothing is "settled" in the area of the determinants of capital structure.

Table 4.5
Capital Structure Determinants—Year 2002
(Long-Term Debt Ratio as Dependent Variable)

$$Y=\beta_0 + \beta_1 AS + \beta_2 GA + \beta_3 NDTS + \beta_4 RFATA + \beta_5 NPM + \beta_6 RD + \beta_7 ADV + \beta_8 SE + \beta_9 CVCF + \beta_{10} CVCF^2 + \beta_{D1} D_1 + \beta_{D2} D_2 + \ldots + \beta_{D18} D_{18} + \varepsilon$$

Independent Variable	Coefficient	t-Value
COCF1	21.9668	0.7186
COCF2	-9.787	2.1131*
Asset	0.0031	0.2884
Growth of Assets	-29.6087	-4.7201**
Depreciation	0.00126	0.3519
Investment Tax Credit	0.01704	0.1986
Fixed Asset Ratio	0.09537	3.2226**
Profit Margin	0.04888	0.6266
R&D Expenditure (%)	-0.64353	-2.1083*
Ad. Expenditure (%)	-0.02662	-0.0713
Selling Expenditure (%)	0.02342	0.2788
Industry Dummy Variables	8 negative 2 positive 8 zero	

* --Significant at the 12% level
**--Significant at the 1% level
Data source: *COMPUSTAT Research Insights* 2003

Table 4.6
Capital Structure Determinants—Year 1992
(Long Term Debt Ratio as Dependent Variable)

$$Y=\beta_0 + \beta_1 AS + \beta_2 GA + \beta_3 NDTS + \beta_4 RFATA + \beta_5 NPM + \beta_6 RD + \beta_7 ADV + \beta_8 SE + \beta_9 CVCF + \beta_{10} CVCF^2 + \beta_{D1} D_1 + \beta_{D2} D_2 + \ldots + \beta_{D18} D_{18} + \varepsilon$$

Independent Variable	Coefficient	t-Value
COCF1	-19.427	-0.4770
COCF2	2.5560	0.3840
Asset	0.0000	0.0610
Growth of Assets	-20.549	-3.2660**
Depreciation	0.0001	0.0320
Investment Tax Credit	-0.0133	-0.1520
Fixed Asset Ratio	0.0993	3.3110**
Profit Margin	-0.0969	-1.2420
R&D Expenditure (%)	-0.8093	-2.6460**
Ad. Expenditure (%)	0.0524	0.1400
Selling Expenditure (%)	-0.0299	-0.3550
Industry Dummy Variables	7 negative 1 positive 10 zero	

* --Significant at the 12% level
**--Significant at the 1% level
Data source: *COMPUSTAT Research Insights* 2002.

References

Harris, M. and R. Raviv, "The Theory of Capital Structure," *Journal of Finance*, 1991, pp. 297-355.

Kale, J.R., T. H. Noe, and G. G. Ramirez, (1991) "The Effect of Business Risk on Corporate Capital Structure: Theory and Evidence," *Journal of Finance* 46, (5), 1693-1715.

Modigliani, F and M. H. Miller, 1958, "The Cost of Capital, Corporation Finance and the Theory of Investment," *American Finance Economic Review* 68, pp. 261-297.

Myers, S., "Determinants of Corporate Borrowing," *Journal of Financial Economics*, Nov. 1977, pp. 147-76.

Myers, Stewart, and Nicholas Majluf, 1984, Corporate Financing and Investment Decisions when Firms Have Information that Investors Do Not Have," *Journal of Financial Economics* 13, pp. 187-221.

Rajan, R.G. and L. Zingales, "What Do We Know about Capital Structure? Some Evidence from International Data," *Journal of Finance*, Dec. 1995, pp. 1421-59.

Smith, Clifford, and Ross Watts, 1992, "The Investment Opportunity Set and Corporate Financing, Dividend and Compensation Policies," *Journal of Financial Economics* 32, pp. 263-292.

Titman, S. and R. Wessels, "The Determinants of Capital Structure Choice," *Journal of Finance*, March 1988, pp. 1-19.

5

Capital Structure and Market Power

Introduction

The financial literature is not unanimous regarding the relationship between capital structure and the market power of firms. While Sullivan (1974), using the data for the period 1956-1963 found a negative relationship between industry concentration (a proxy for market power) and debt ratios, Melicher, Rush and Winn (1999), using data from 1965-1974 found no relationship between industry concentration and debt ratios. But Lyn and Papaioannou (1998), using more recent census data, found that firms in high concentration industries, respond to changes in factors that affect debt policy with greater restraint when setting their debt ratios, that is, negative relationship between industry concentration and debt ratios.

In order to make inferences about the financing policies of firms that differ in market power, we have to make a clear distinction between competitive and monopolistic firms. Monopolistic firms operate in highly concentrated industries; they produce goods of low substitutability; they employ highly specialized resources with illiquid secondary markets and large mobility costs; and finally they possess exclusive future investment opportunities. Competitive firms, on the other hand, produce goods that have easy substitutes in the products of other firms in the same industry; and they employ non-specialized and thus easily transferable resources with liquid secondary markets. Although such firms can possess future investment opportunities, other firms can easily exploit these opportunities. We use these different characteristics in order to argue that the size of expected bankruptcy costs are different between competitive and monopolistic firms.

The market superiority of monopolistic firms rests on exclusive product features resulting from such production and marketing techniques that a firm would either decline to reveal or it would be costly to communicate to the market. Therefore, it is plausible to argue that information asymmetry is normally greater for the future cash flows of monopolistic firms than it is for competitive firms. Consequently, the Myers-Majluf type of external financing costs will be larger for monopolistic firms than it will be for competitive firms. Thus, differences in the real factors of firms cause the monopolist to have significant bankruptcy related costs which must offset other benefits from borrowing. Therefore, one would predict that, other things being equal, an optimal debt ratio will be reached at a lower level for a monopolistic firm than it will for a competitive firm.

This chapter will reexamine the question whether firms differing in market power have different debt ratios. We expect that firms with specialized and less mobile resources that operate in highly concentrated industries are prone to incur larger bankruptcy costs than firms with a low degree of industry concentration. Similarly, firms with higher market power will issue less debt to finance future investment options, using more retained earnings, as Myers (1984) has suggested in his Pecking Order Theory of capital structure. Moreover, when we examine the relationship between financial slack (cash and equivalents) and industry concentration, we expect that with increased industry concentration, firms have a tendency to build up their financial slacks which can serve as debt capacity in reserve, as Lyn and Papaioannou have found.

The hypothesis we will test is whether firms in the higher concentrated industries have lower debt ratios, as the majority of the studies suggest. The explanatory variables we will be using should be able to discern the nature as well as the magnitude of this relationship to be found in the United States industries in 1992 as well as in 2002. This study, thus, will delve into an important area of capital structure research. Although this kind of study had been done before, this research project in this area will be significantly different on three counts. First, this is the first time that the same firms will be studied for their degree of industry concentration and debt ratios as was studied by Ghosh and Cai (1999) for their optimal capital structure before in the broad framework of capital structure analysis. Second, we will apply more relevant explanatory variables not used before. And third, we will bring the subject matter up-to-date by examining the latest industry concentration ratios as found in the *2002 Concentration in the Manufacturing Industries Census* data.

Data Source and Methodology

The data source for the concentration ratios of the United States manufacturing industries are the 1992 and 2002 editions of the *Concentration Ratios in Manufacturing*, issued by the U.S. Department of Commerce.

Each of the establishments, covered in the 1992 and 2002 *Economic Census-Manufacturing*, was classified in one of 480 industries (473 manufacturing industries and seven former manufacturing industries) in accordance with the industry definitions in the 1997 *NAICS manuals*. This is the first edition of the *NAICS Manual* and it is a major change from the *1987 SIC Manual* that was used previously.

In the NAICS system, an industry is generally defined as a group of establishments that have a similar production process. To the extent practical, the system uses supply-based or production-oriented concepts in defining industries. The resulting group of establishments must be significant in terms of number, value-added by manufacture, value of shipments, and number of employees. In the manufacturing sector for 2002, there are 21 sub-sectors (three-digit NAICS), 86 industry groups (four-digit NAICS), 184 NAICS industries (five-digit NAICS) that are comparable with Canadian and Mexican classifications, and 473 U.S. industries (six-digit NAICS). This represents an expansion of the four-digit SIC-based U.S. industries from 459 in 1987.

As for corporate financial records, we will rely on the *COMPUSTAT* database. To explain the relationship between industry concentration and debt ratios of firms, we will use operating profits as well as the variability of profits as explanatory variables. Operating profits should measure the ability of firms to finance with retained earnings and thus avoid external financing through debt. In this case, the relationship of operating profitability and the debt ratio will be negative. Variability of profits, on the other hand, has been found to have an ambiguous relationship with the debt ratio. In addition to these variables, we will employ the ratio of market value of equity to its book value (Tobin's Q-ratio), as the proxy for future investment opportunities. In general, a lower debt ratio is associated with fewer future investment options. Consequently, the Q-ratio should be negatively correlated with the debt ratio.

We will classify our sample into six groups of firms in ascending order of their concentration ratios. Within each group we will run simple regressions of the debt ratio on each of the explanatory variables as follows:

$$DEBTj = a0 + a1\ OPRj$$
$$DEBTj = b0 + b1\ VOPRj$$
$$DEBTj = c0 + c1\ QRj$$

Where:

DEBT = the ratio of current and long-term debt to total assets;
OPR = the ratio of EBIT to total assets;
VOPR = standard deviation of OPR;
QR = the ratio of market value of equity to its book value;
J = a firm identification subscript.

If bankruptcy costs increase as we move to groups with higher industry concentration, we will expect to see a diminishing contribution of each independent variable to debt. That is, the regression coefficients a1, b1, and c1 should decline in size as we move from group #1 to group #6 (to higher industry concentration).

As for financial slack (cash and its equivalents), we can hypothesize that the factors which affect debt ratios negatively should affect financial slack positively. Thus for each group of firms, we run the simple regression models:

SLACKj = a0 + a1 OPRj;
SLACKj = b0 + b1 VCPRj;
SLACKj = c0 + c1 QRj

Where:

SLACK = the ratio of cash and equivalents to current and long-term debt.

The prediction is that the contribution of the independent variables to SLACK increases as we move to groups of firms with higher industry concentration.

Empirical Results

In table 5.1A, we have shown the number of firms belonging to each concentration class, along with the average concentration ratio of that group for 1992. We find that 50 percent of the sample total belonged to the lowest concentration class, namely, the 8-27 percent group, while the second largest number belonged to the highest concentration class, namely, the 60-93 percent group. Also, the number of firms were the same (7) for both the 28-35 percent concentration class and the 53-59 percent concentration class. The average 4-firm concentration ratio in the lowest class was only 18.23 percent, while for the highest class, it was 74.31 percent.

Table 5.1A
Descriptive Statistics of Concentration Ratios in U.S. Manufacturing Industries, 1992

Concentration Group	Number of Firms	Average 4-firm Concentration (%)
1. 8 – 27%	52	18.23
2. 28 – 35%	7	30.97
3. 36 – 47%	11	42.14
4. 48 – 52%	9	49.75
5. 53 – 59%	7	56.54
6. 60 – 93%	13	74.31
	Total = 99	Average = 45.32

Table 5.1B
Descriptive Statistics of Concentration Ratios in U.S. Manufacturing Industries, 2002

Concentration Group	Number of Firms	Average 4-firm Concentration (%)
1. 8 -27%	71	20.9
2. 28 -35%	107	32.3
3. 36 -47%	142	38.9
4. 48 – 52%	94	50.3
5. 53 – 59%	7	55.0
6. 60 – 93%	43	76.6
	Total = 464	Average = 45.67

But in table 5.1B for the 2002 sample, 31 percent of the firms belonged to the 36–47 percent concentration class, with the 27-35 percent concentration class having the next largest group of firms. The percentage of firms belonging to the highest concentration class (59-93 percent) increased slightly in 2002 as compared to 1992, which was also true for the lowest concentration class (8-27 percent). In total, 74 percent of the firms belonged to the three classes in the middle range in 2002, while the largest percentage of firms belonged to the lowest concentration class in 1992.

In table 5.2, we have calculated the univariate regressions using a firm's debt ratio as the dependent variable, and operating profit (OPR), variability of operating ratio (VOPR) and Tobin's Q-ratio (QR) as the independent variables for 1992. Here we find that the β-coefficients representing operating profit ratio have negative signs in five of the six

Table 5.2
Univariate Regression of Debt on OPR, VOPR, and QR, Respectively, 1992

Concentration Class	Intercept	OPR	Intercept	VOPR	Intercept	QR
8-27%	0.2709	0.0083	0.2314	0.7471*	0.2660	0.0080
		(0.5301)		(2.4883)		(0.5240)
28-35%	0.2865	-0.0598	0.1848	-0.3680**	0.2805	-0.0598
		(0.3335)		(-1.7528)		(0.2893)
36-47%	0.2553	-0.2752*	0.2174	0.3310*	0.2494	0.0358
		(2.8936)		(2.9685)		(0.2559)
48-52%	0.2887	-0.2337	0.2252	0.5103	0.2651	-0.0078
		(0.1305)		(0.1472)		(0.1607)
53-59%	0.2758	-0.3201*	0.3441	-1.1068	0.2644	-0.0132
		(3.3205)		(0.3386)		(0.3469)
60 – 93%	0.3570	-0.9203*	0.2819	-0.8933	0.2910	- 0.2153*
		(3.3591)		(0.2380)		(-3.2936)

*t-values significant at the 1% level.
**t-values significant at the 5% level.

regressions, out of which the t-values are significant for three equations. Also, they are in descending order with higher concentration ratios, as expected by the null hypothesis. But for the variability of operating profits (VOPR), only three of the six equations have negative signs, and also t-values of three b-coefficients are significant, either at the 1 percent level or at the 5 percent level. As for Tobin's Q-ratio, four equations have negative signs as expected by the theory, and only one has the t-value significant at the 1 percent level.

In table 5., we have calculated the univariate regression equations using the debt ratio as the dependent variable, and operating profits (OPR), variability of operating profits (VOPR), and Tobin's Q-ratio (QR) as the independent variables for 2000. We find that the β-coefficients for the operating profit ratio (OPR) have negative signs in five out of six regression equations, as in table 5.2. Here, also, the t-values are significant in three out of the six equations. But the β-coefficients are not in exactly descending order with higher concentration ratios, as seen in table 5.2 and as predicted by the null hypothesis. For the variability of operating profits (VOPR), only three of the six equations have negative signs, and t-values are significant at the 5 percent level in only two equations. As for Tobin's Q-ratio, three equations have negative signs with their t-values significant at the 5 percent level.

Table 5.3
Univariate Regression of Debt on OPR, VOPR, and QR, Respectively, for 2002

Concentration Class	Intercept	OPR	Intercept	VOPR	Intercept	QR
1. 8-27%	0.202	0.213	0.203	-0.001	0.175	0.001
		(1.31)		(-0.53)		(0.53)
2. 28-35%	0.184	-0.263*	0.115	0.462*	0.197	-0.008**
		(-2.97)		(2.42)		(-1.86)
3. 36-47%	0.253	-0.072	0.266	-0.135	0.245	-0.003**
		(-0.76)		(-0.53)		(1.72)
4. 48-52%	0.187	-0.214*	0.190	0.027	0.171	-0.003**
		(-3.00)		(0.22)		(1.92)
5. 53-59%	0.304	-0.478	0.342	-1.65*	0.250	0.007
		(-0.66)		(-2.22)		(0.20)
6. 60-93%	0.359	-1.05*	0.251	0.886	0.282	0.001
		(-3.01)		(1.23)		(1.72)

*t-values significant at the 0.01% level.
** t-values significant at the 0.05% level.

Table 5.4
Univariate Regression of Slack Variable on OPR, VOPR, and QR, Respectively, 1992

Concentration Class	Intercept	OPR	Intercept	VOPR	Intercept	QR
8-27%	0.1941	0.7984**	0.2701	0.0083	0.2663	0.0086
		(1.2191)		(0.5477)		(0.5241)
28-35%	0.3215	0.2984	0.3215	-0.2584*	0.2865	-0.0598
		(0.3256)		(2.8572)		(0.3335)
36-47%	0.2563	0.2752**	0.2558	-0.2752	0.2651	-0.0078
		(1.9356)		(0.2327)		(0.1622)
48-52%	0.2651	0.0078	0.2651	-0.0157	0.2386	0.0085
		(0.1622)		(0.1606)		(0.5839)
53-59%	0.2844	0.0132*	0.2643	-0.0132	0.2569	-0.1334*
		(2.6749)		(0.3469)		(2.7239)
60-93%	0.2910	0.2153*	0.3637	0.2133*	0.2493	0.1513*
		(2.3586)		(2.8622)		(2.8381)

*t-values significant at the 0.01% level.
**t-values significant at the 0.05% level.

In table 5.4, we have shown the regression results when the slack variable (cash and equivalents) was the dependent variable, and operating profits ratio(OPR), variability of operating profits ratio (VOPR), and Tobin's Q-ratio were the independent variables for the 1992 census data. Here we find that all the coefficients for operating profits ratio are positive, as the theory would suggest. And four out of the six equations have t-values significant either at the 0.01 percent level or at the 0.05 percent level. For the variability of operating profits ratio as the independent variable, four equations have negative signs, but only two are significant at the 1 percent level. For the equations representing Tobin's Q-ratio as the independent variable, only three out of the six equations have positive signs, but only two equations have the t-values significant at the 1 percent level.

Table 5.5 shows the regression results for 2002 when the slack variable (cash and equivalents) is the dependent variable. Here also four equations have positive signs when the operating profit ratio (OPR) is the independent variable. But only two equations have significant t-values either at the 1 percent or at the 10 percent level. As for VOPR as the independent variable, all of them have positive signs, with four of the six equations having significant t-values at the 1 percent or at the 5 percent level. For the equations taking QR as the independent variable, four out of the six

Table 5.5
Univariate Regression of Slack Variable on OPR, VOPR, and QR, Respectively
2002

Concentration Class	Intercept	OPR	Intercept	VOPR	Intercept	QR
1. 8-27%	0.159	0.396*	0.151	0.001	0.153	0.002***
		(3.69)		(0.87)		(1.39)
2. 28-35%	0.158	-0.087***	0.152	0.044	0.165	0.003
		(-1.46)		(0.51)		(1.16)
3. 36-47%	0.114	0.028	0.080	0.373*	0.120	0.001
		(0.72)		(3.82)		(0.80)
4. 48-52%	0.163	-0.61	0.143	0.163**	0.171	-0.001
		(-1.02)		(1.83)		(-1.23)
5. 53-59%	0.592	0.086	-0.002	1.432*	0.049	0.006***
		(0.25)		(3.27)		(1.45)
6. 60-93%	0.091	0.002	0.068	0.332**	0.086	-0.001
		(0.02)		(1.84)		(0.75)

* Significant at the 1% level.
** Significant at the 5% level.
*** Significant at the 10% level.

equations have positive signs, as the theory suggests, but only two have t-values significant at the 0.10 percent level.

In table 5.6, we have employed a multiple regression analysis for the 1992 census data. Here Sales have a negative impact on the debt ratio in four concentration classes, but Assets have a positive impact in four out of six concentration classes. Selling expenses have three positive signs out of the six concentration classes, but the operating profit ratio (EBIT) has four negative signs in six classes. Cash and equivalents, however, have negative signs in all of the six classes, which is also true for R & D expenditures. However, except for the intercepts and for one concentration class for Cash and equivalents, the t-values are not significant in any level. The low R^2 and F-values bear this out.

In table 5.7, we have also employed a multiple regression analysis for the 2002 concentration data. Here Sales has a negative impact on the debt

Table 5.6
Multiple Regression Analysis of Firm Capital Structure & Concentration Class, 1992

Industry Conc. (%)	8-27	28-35	36-47	48-52	53-59	60-93
Intercept	.230c	.183c	.204c	.174c	.138b	.277c
(t value)	(9.39)	(6.77)	(10.4)	(4.37)	(2.57)	(3.56)
Sales (x104)	-.261	-.464	-1.07	-.410	2.66	.163
	(-0.36)	(-0.18)	(-0.31)	(-0.12)	(1.44)	(0.46)
Assets (x103)	.184	.197	.021	-.085	-.034	.034
	(1.28)	(0.81)	(0.84)	(-0.23)	(-0.14)	(0.93)
Selling Exp. (x103)	-.129	1.01	.040	1.72	-.202	-.021
	(-0.27)	(1.06)	(0.42)	(1.06)	(-0.16)	(-0.42)
EBIT (x103)	-.848	-1.60	-.080	1.15	-1.92	.087
	(-1.04)	(-1.32)	(-0.57)	(0.73)	(-0.92)	(0.54)
Cash & Eq. (x103)	-.458	-.528	-.019	-2.34**	-.274	-.103
	(-0.82)	(-0.85)	(-0.20)	(-1.72)	(-0.09)	(-0.99)
R & D (x103)	-.450	-3.97	-.205	-5.38	-.219	-.639
	(-0.20)	(-1.47)	(-0.78)	(-1.33)	(-0.05)	(-0.83)
F	0.47	0.96	0.67	1.01	1.07	0.27
R2	.02	.05	.03	.01	.02	.07
N	161	112	157	21	22	27

*t-values significant at the 10% level.
**t-values significant at the 5% level.

ratio in only two of the five (we could not use the regression equation for the 53-59 concentration class due to the paucity of the number of firms) concentration classes. But Assets are positively correlated with the debt ratio in four out of the five equations. So also is the Selling Expense which has positive signs in four out of the five equations. But, just like table 5.6, EBIT has four negative signs. Cash and equivalents also have four negative signs, while R & D expenditures have three positive signs out of the five concentration classes. Here also, the t-values were significant for the intercepts and only one concentration class for Selling Expenses. The low R^2 as well as the F-ratio indicate rather poor correlation of the independent variables with the dependent variable.

Concluding Remarks

Our study has shown that there is no meaningful relationship between industrial concentration and capital structure. This result was corroborated

Table 5.7
Multiple Regression Analysis of Firm Capital Structure & Concentration Class, 2002

Industry Conc. (%)	8-27	28-35	36-47	47-52	53-59	60-93
Intercept	0.191	0.182	0.243	0.176	--	0.312
	(1.23)					
Sales	0.317**	0.121	-0.002	0.003	--	-0.115
	(2.07)	(0.39)	(-0.12)	(0.48)	--	(1.08)
Assets	-0.009	0.001	0.011	0.010	--	0.007
	(-1.01)	(0.00)	(0.54)	(0.80)	--	(1.04)
Selling Exp.	-0.895**	0.029	0.007	0.021	--	0.005
	(-2.16)	(0.13)	(0.11)	(0.40)	--	(0.20)
EBIT	-0.442	-0.030	-0.029	0.040	--	-0.004
	(-1.14)	(-0.13)	(-0.37)	(0.70)		(-0.22)
Cash & Eqv.	0.061	-0.014	-0.047	-0.099	--	-0.020
	(0.26)	(-0.24)	(-0.33)	(-1.84)	--	(-0.39)
R & D Exp.	0.434	-0.132	-0.057	0.003	--	0.107
	(0.55)	(-0.41)	(-0.21)	(0.02)		(0.60)
F-ratio	1.69	0.17	0.22	1.99	--	0.33
R^2	0.06	0.01	0.01	0.22	--	0.05
N	71	107	142	94	7	43

* t-values significant at the 5% level.

by Melicher, Rush and Winn in an earlier study. Also, no relation was found between differing concentration ratios and different debt ratios by industries. Furthermore, the regression analyses show no significant relationship among the debt ratios and operating incomes in descending order by higher concentration classes. This is also true when the slack variable was used as the dependent variable.

References

Ghosh, A. and F. Cai. "Capital Structure: New Evidence of Optimality and Pecking Order Theory." *American Business Review*, 1999.

Lyn, E. and G. Papaioannou. "The Empirical Relationship between Capital Structure and Market Power." *Working Paper,* 1998.

Melicher, R. W., D. F. Rush, and D.W. Winn. "Industry Concentration, Financial Structure and Profitability." *Financial Management,* 1999, 5, 48-59.

Myers, S. C. "The Capital Structure Puzzle." *Journal of Finance*, 1984, 39, 575-592.

Sullivan, T. G. "Market Power, Profitability and Financial Leverage." *Journal of Finance*, 1974, 24, 3-18.

6

New Stock Offerings and Stockholders' Returns

Because of asymmetric information, the traditional finance theory suggests that for external financing, firms with good future prospects prefer to finance with debt, while firms with poor prospects like to finance with common stocks (Brigham and Eherhardt, 2003). Thus the announcement of a stock offering is generally taken as a signal that the firm's prospects as seen by its management are not bright. This, in turn, suggests that when a firm announces a new stock offering, more often than not, the price of its stock will decline. Empirical studies have verified this hypothesis (Asquith and Mullins, Jr., 1983).

Thus the signaling effect of new stock issues is that the investors recognize this weakness, so the selling pressure drives down a company's share price when it announces a plan to issue new shares. The *SEC Monthly Statistical Review* also shows that historically the U.S. firms undertake equity financing far less than debt financing. The data also seem to indicate that firms prefer to issue equity when the stock price is relatively high, as observed by Marsh (Marsh, 1982). Marsh also found that "smaller firms, those with few fixed assets, and those with greater bankruptcy risk are more likely to issue equity"(*Ibid*).

More recently, Ronald Masulis had summarized the empirical studies regarding debt/equity choice and reported that announcements of security offerings consistently were greeted with nonpositive stock price response, even though these corporate decisions were voluntary and presumably were associated with profitable investment projects (Masulis, 1988). He further reported that when common stocks were issued, there was a negative announcement return of 3.3 percent, but when the opposite capital structure change is announced—namely, a tender offer to repurchase stock—there was a large announcement return of 16.4 percent.

In this chapter, we address the same problem anew, namely, whether new issues of stock by an existing firm depresses its stock price after the announcement date, and thus results in negative returns to its stockholders. There are three main contributions of our analysis. First, we have collected data from 1990 to1997 when the stock market was quite bullish. Second, we have divided our data set into stocks, which were listed in the New York Stock Exchange (NYSE) and in the over-the-counter market (NASDAQ), in order to examine whether the returns were significantly different because of firms belonging to these two separate markets. Finally, we have also divided the 1990-1997 time period into two sub-periods—1990 to 1993 when the stock market was mildly bullish and 1994-1997 when the market was highly bullish, the purposes being to capture the difference in the degree of bull markets as well as the impact of difference in stock market organizations during the last decade.

Data Source and Methodology

For the announcement dates of new stock issues by different companies, we have used the *Wall Street Journal* Index of various issues covering the time period 1990-1997. For the calculation of the returns of the stocks, we have used the CRSP data files of daily returns covering the same period. The research methodology we follow is that of "event" studies. Ever since the path-breaking article published by Fama, Fisher, Jensen, and Roll concerning their study of the announcement of stock splits (Fama, et al., 1969), event study methodology has been used extensively for calculating the impact on stock prices and stock returns of new market issues, exchange listings, announcement of accounting changes, annual and quarterly earnings reports, depreciation and inventory changes, and mergers and acquisitions, among other factors. The basic assumption of the event study methodology is the Efficient Market Hypothesis (EMH) of the semistrong form, which asserts that security prices adjust rapidly to the release of all new public information (the weak form assumes the current stock prices fully reflect all stock market information, while the strong form contends that stock prices fully reflect all information, public or otherwise).

There are generally two ways of calculating average abnormal returns (AAR)—the "market" model and the "comparison period" model. The unique relationship between a stock and the market returns for a period prior to and subsequent to a significant economic event can be calculated with the help of Standard & Poor's market index of 500 common stocks. There are quite a few varieties of market models, a good description of which can be found in Brown and Warner (Brown and Warner, 1980).

The comparison period approach was used very successfully by Brown and Warner to compute abnormal returns (*Ibid*). This study has shown that the comparison period approach works as well as the more sophisticated market model in detecting abnormal performance when it is present. In this study, we have used the comparison period model. To determine the daily abnormal return of a security, we first calculate the average daily return over a specified interval—the comparison period. This comparison period return (CPR) is taken as an estimate of the expected daily return for the period under study—the "observation period." The CPR for our comparison period calculation was based on the average daily returns from day –17 through day –7, and from day +7 through day +17—altogether 24 days' average. The observation period extends from day –6 through day +6—a period of 13 crucial days.

A t-statistic that tests whether the average abnormal return for day m is significantly different than zero is calculated, following Jain (Jain 1985), by:

$$Tm = AARm/s$$

Where s is the estimated standard deviation of the AARs, calculated from the comparison period relative to the event days for each firm. Similarly, the t-statistic of CAAR for a period of n days from day a to day b is calculated by:

$$Tab = CAARab/s\hat{}1/2n$$

Empirical Results

In table 6.1, we have shown the daily average abnormal returns (AAR) and the cumulative average abnormal returns (CAAR) of our sample of 50 firms around the announcement dates of new stock offerings. Here we find that on the announcement day, the return of all firms was –0.0735 or –7.35 percent, as was –5.91 percent on the prior day of announcement. During the observation period, the average abnormal return was negative for 9 out of 13 days.

When we calculate the cumulative average abnormal returns (CAAR) over selected intervals for all firms under study, as shown in table 6.2, we find that for the entire 13-day observation period, the cumulative average abnormal returns was –0.1147 or –11.47 percent. It was -10.11 percent

Table 6.1
Daily Average Abnormal Returns (AAR) and Cumulative Average Abnormal Returns (CAAR) of Firms Around the Announcement Date
All Firms, 1990 – 1997

Days	AAR	t-statistic	CARR
-6	0.0640	3.1123***	0.0640
-5	-0.0469	-2.9303**	0.0171
-4	-0.0301	-1.9806**	0.0130
-3	-0.0745	-4.1239***	0.0875
-2	0.0455	2.8729**	-0.0420
-1	-0.0591	-3.0102**	-0.1011
0	-0.0735	-4.0235***	-0.1786
+1	0.1310	5.3693***	-0.0436
+2	-0.0441	-2.6304**	-0.0877
+3	-0.0117	1.3235*	-0.0994
+4	-0.0414	-2.5277**	-0.1408
+5	-0.0617	-3.0801***	-0.2025
+6	0.0878	4.5353***	-0.1147

* Significant at the 10% level.
** Significant at the 5% level.
*** Significant at the 1% level.

Table 6.2
Cumulative Average Abnormal Returns Over Selected Intervals,
All Firms, 1990 - 1997

Intervals	CAAR	t-statistic
-6 day through +6 day	-0.1147	-4.3692***
-6 day through -1 day	-0.1011	-4.1819***
-1 day through day 0	-0.1326	-5.3892***
+2 day through +6 day	-0.0711	-3.9783***

*** Significant at the 1% level.

cumulatively for 6 days prior to the announcement date, as was –7.11% for the period of day +2 through day +6. It was –13.26% for the most crucial period of day –1 through day 0.

When we divide our sample firms into the firms belonging to the New York Stock Exchange (NYSE) and the firms belonging to the over-the-counter market (OTC), as shown in table 6.3, we find that on the announcement day, the AAR of the NYSE firms were –0.1660 or –16.60 percent, while the AAR for the OTC firms was 0.0890 or 8.90 percent, respectively. For the entire observation period, the CAAR was –0.3973 or –39.73 percent, but for the OTC firms, it was 11.88 percent.

Table 6.3
Daily Average Abnormal Returns (AAR) and Cumulative Average Abnormal Returns (CAAR) Around the Announcement Date for NYSE and OTC Firms

	NYSE Firms			OTC Firms	
Days	AAR	CAAR	Days	AAR	CAAR
-6	-0.0865	-0.0865	-6	0.2370	0.2370
-5	-0.1651	-0.2516	-5	0.0755	0.3125
-4	-0.0781	-0.3297	-4	0.0023	0.3148
-3	-0.2304	-0.5601	-3	0.0151	0.2997
-2	-0.0048	-0.5649	-2	0.0996	0.3993
-1	-0.1338	-0.6987	-1	0.0017	0.4010
0	-0.1660	-0.8647	0	0.1069	0.5079
+1	0.1729	-0.6918	+1	0.0890	0.5969
+2	-0.0936	-0.7854	+2	0.0293	0.5676
+3	0.1139	-0.6715	+3	-0.1669	0.4007
+4	-0.0257	-0.6972	+4	0.0618	0.3389
+5	0.1203	-0.5769	+5	0.1802	0.1587
+6	0.1796	-0.3973	+6	0.0399	0.1188

Obviously, the NASDAQ market, being more robust and dominated by relatively smaller capitalization firms, shrugged off the adverse effect of new stock offerings by the existing firms during 1990-1997.

In table 6.4, we have shown the CAAR over selected intervals for both the NYSE and the OTC firms. Here the pattern was more pronounced. The CAAR of the NYSE firms for day -6 through day –1 was –0.6987 or –69.87 percent, but for the OTC firms during the same period, it was 0.4010 or 40.10 percent. Even for the crucial period of day –1 through day 0, the CAAR for the NYSE firms was –29.98 percent, but for the OTC firms it was 10.86 percent. But the reverse was true when we calculate the CAAR for day +2 through day +6. For the NYSE firms it was 29.45 percent, but for the OTC firms, it was –47.81 percent.

Table 6.4
Cumulative Average Abnormal Returns Over Selected Intervals, NYSE and OTC Firms, 1990 – 1997

	NYSE Firms			OTC Firms	
Interval	CAAR	t-stat.	Interval	CAAR	t-stat
-6 through +6	-0.3973	-6.7892***	-6 through +6	0.1188	4.3735***
-6 through –1	-0.6987	-8.3124***	-6 through –1	0.4010	6.8193***
-1 through 0	-0.2998	5.8257***	-1 through 0	0.1086	4.0256***
+2 through +6	0.2945	5.6931***	+2 through +6	-0.4781	7.8112***

*** Significant at the 1% level.

In table 6.5, we have divided our sample firms into two sub-periods, namely, 1990-1993 that we may characterize as mildly bullish, and 1994-1997 which was strongly bullish. Here we find that during the 1990-1993 time period, the average abnormal returns from day -6 through day 0 were all negative, but those from day +1 through day +6, except for day +4, were positive. The reverse was true for the period 1994-1997 when, except for day –3, the average abnormal returns of all the other days before and including the event date were positive. But they were negative from day +1 through day +5.

When we calculate the CAAR, as shown in table 6.6, the results were more pronounced for these two subperiods. During the 1990-1993 period, the CAAR for the crucial days of –1 through 0, was –0.3267, while for the 1994-1997 time period it was 0.0864. Also, for the days covering –6 through –2, the CAAR during 1990-1993 was –0.5570, while it was 0.3030 for the same days during. Similarly, the CAAR for the entire observation period was –0.5663 for 1990-1993, while it was 0.1711 for 1994-1997. Obviously, during the mildly stock market bullish period of 1990-1993, the average abnormal returns were negative as the finance theory suggested, but they were positive during 1994-1997 when the market was extremely bullish and the economy was unusually robust.

Table 6.5
Daily Average Abnormal Returns and Cumulative Average Abnormal Returns Around the Announcement Date During 1990-1993 and 1994-1997

1990 – 1993			1994 – 1997		
Days	AAR	CAAR	Days	AAR	CAAR
-6	-0.0350	-0.0350	-6	0.1219	0.1219
-5	-0.1933	-0.2283	-5	0.0932	0.2151
-4	-0.0845	-0.3128	-4	0.0536	0.2687
-3	-0.1421	-0.4549	-3	-0.1976	0.0711
-2	-0.1021	-0.5570	-2	0.2321	0.3032
-1	-0.1381	-0.6951	-1	0.0453	0.3485
0	-0.1886	-0.8837	0	0.0411	0.3896
+1	0.2286	-0.6551	+1	-0.0380	0.3396
+2	0.0160	-0.6391	+2	-0.0380	0.3396
+3	0.0411	-0.5980	+3	-0.1076	0.2320
+4	-0.0825	-0.6805	+4	-0.0483	0.2237
+5	0.0582	-0.6223	+5	-0.1302	0.0935
+6	0.0560	-0.5663	+6	0.0776	0.1711

Table 6.6
Cumulative Average Abnormal Returns Over Selected Intervals

1990 – 1993			1994 – 1997		
Interval	CAAR	t-stat.	Interval	CAAR	t-stat.
-6 through +6	-0.5663	7.9327***	-6 through +6	0.1711	4.8983***
-6 through –1	-0.6951	-8.2922***	-6 through –1	0.3485	6.0120***
-1 through 0	-0.3267	-5.9891***	-1 through 0	0.0864	3.5439***
+2 through +6	0.3174	-5.7328***	+2 through +6	0.2465	5.3137***

***Significant at the 1% level.

We have also fitted the OLS regression model to the data to calculate the association between the average abnormal return and the determining factors. The regression equation may be described as follows:

AAR = a0 + b1DTA + b2LTA + b3GRS + b4Dumvar

Where:

AAR = Average Abnormal Returns during the Event Days –1 through +1;
DTA = Total Debt/Total Assets;
LTA = Log of Total Assets;
GRS = One-year growth Rate of Sales;
DumVer = Dummy variable equal to 1 if the firm was listed in the NYSE, otherwise 0.

The results are shown in table 6.7. Here we find that the average during the three event days was negatively associated with the debt ratio, as higher debt would lead to lower abnormal return. The t-value of the β-coefficient of this variable was also significant at the 5 percent level. Similarly, the average abnormal return was also statistically significant for the dummy variable, indicating that it was significant whether the stock was listed in the New York Stock Exchange or in the OTC market.

Unfortunately, total assets as well as growth of sales were not significant at all at any level. But the strong negative association between the average abnormal return and the debt/asset ratio confirms that capital structure matters, that is, firms' decision regarding the form of external financing, will have direct impact on the abnormal returns during the event period.

Table 6.7
OLS Regression Analysis with Average Abnormal Returns (AAR) of the Event Days (-1 through +1) As the Dependent Variable

Independent Variable	Intercept	β-coefficients	t-values
	a_0 = -0.0203		
DTA		-0.0820	-2.5761*
LTA		0.0010	0.2867
GRS		0.0001	0.3206
DumVar		0.0235	1.4406**
N = 41			
R2 = 0.2501			
F = 3.0010			

* Significant at the 5% level.
** Significant at the 10% level.

Concluding Remarks

Our event study has shown that the average abnormal return of firms belonging to the NYSE on the day of announcement of substantial amount of new stock offerings was -16.60 percent and the cumulative average abnormal return for the observation period was -39.73 percent. But for firms belonging to the OTC market, the average abnormal return was 8.90 percent on the announcement date, while for the cumulative average abnormal return it was 11.88 percent. Also, the average abnormal return on the announcement date was negative during 1990-1993, but was positive during 1994-1997. It seems that the adverse effect of new stock offerings on stock returns was more pronounced for the established well-capitalized NYSE firms than for the newer and smaller capitalized firms in the NASDAQ market. We should also remember that the strong bull market of the late 1990s was able to negate the generally adverse impact of new stock offerings on the stock return of firms.

References

Asquith, P and D. Mullins, Jr. (1983). The Impact of Initiating Dividend Payments on Shareholders' Wealth, *Journal of Business*, 56 (1), 77-96.

Brav, A. (2000). Is the Abnormal Return Following Equity Issuance Anomalous? *Journal of Financial Economics*, 56 (2), 209-36.

Brigham, E. F. and M. C. Eherhardt (2003). *Financial Management: Theory and Practice*, Dryden Press, 10th ed., 662-690.

Brous, P. A. (1994). The Valuation Effects of Equity Issues and the Level of Institutional Ownership: Evidence from Analysts' Earnings Forecasts, *Financial Management*, 23 (1), 33-45.

Brown, S. J., and J. B. Warner (1980). Measuring Security Price Performance, *Journal of Financial Economics*, 8 (2), 205-258.

Denis, D. A. (1994). Investment Opportunities and the Market Reaction to Equity Offerings, *Journal of Financial and Quantitative Analysis*, 29 (2), 159-178.

Fama, E.F., L. Fisher, M. C. Jensen, and R. Roll (1969). The Adjustment of Stock Prices to New Information, *International Economic Review*, 10 (1), 1-21.

Jain, P. (1985). The Effect of Voluntary Sell-Off Announcements on Shareholders' Wealth, *Journal of Finance*, 40 (1), 209-24.

Lee, W. W. (1998). A Free Cash Flow Explanation for the Wealth Effect of Seasoned Equity Offerings, *American Business Review*, 16 (2), 100-109.

Loughran, T. (1997). The Operating Performance of Firms Conducting Seasoned Equity Offerings, *Journal of Finance*, 52 (5), 1823-51.

Marsh, P. (1982). The Choice between Equity and Debt: An Empirical Study, *Journal of Finance*, 37 (1), 121-44.

Masulis, R. (1988). *The Debt/Equity Choice*, Cambridge: M. A. Ballinger Publishing Co.

McLaughlin, T. (1996). The Operating Performance of Seasoned Equity Issuers: Free Cash Flow and Post-Issue Performance, *Financial Management*, 25 (4), 41-54.

Roni, M. (1995). The Choice of Going Public: Spin-Offs vs. Carve-Outs, *Financial Management*, 24 (3), 5-22.

Wu, C. (2001). The Price Behavior of Seasoned Equities around the Offering Date, *Journal of Business & Economic Studies*, 7 (2), 14-26.

7

Capital Structure and Executive Compensation

Capital structure of firms has been associated with new stock offerings, ownership structure, market power, and business risks, among others. Capital structure changes have been associated with firm size, growth of sales, depreciation, fixed asset ratios, profit margin, R & D expenditures, advertising, and selling expenditures as explanatory variables (Ghosh and Cai, 2000). Shedidan Titman also found uniqueness (such as the rate at which employees voluntarily leave their job) as the significant variable to explain the changes in capital structure (Titman, 1988).

Similarly, executive compensation of major U.S. firms has been associated with ownership and firm performance (Mehran, 1995), corporate investment and financing decisions (Agrawal and Mandelker, 1987), the threat of takeovers (Agrawal and Knoeber, 1998), managerial compensation and incentives (Baker, et al., 1988), among others. Recently, R. L. Simarly, Minfang Li, and K. E. Bass, in an unpublished article, have explored the relationship between CEO compensation and the economic performance of the U.S. firms contributing to the global competitiveness, which, in turn, has enhanced the economic benefits for all (Fisher, 1998).

In this chapter we want to explore the relationship between capital structure and executive compensation, not examined directly before, although Mehran had incorporated some of these ideas in his works. The hypothesis to be tested is that when a firm issues bonds, it generally uses the proceeds for investment opportunities and further expansion of the production process, as a result of which profits would increase and so would the stockholders' returns. Therefore, with the eventual increase of stock price when the profit is higher, the executive compensation would increase as a reward for the expansion of the business and higher profitability.

Thus we will expect a positive and statistically significant correlation between the salary and bonus, or total compensation (including stock options) of the CEOs of major corporations in the United States, and the debts these companies incurred during the period covered by our study. As other explanatory variables, we may use size of firms, sales growth, net income, and stock price returns. We may also use the dummy variables as industry characteristics to be related with executive compensations. All these independent variables should be positively associated with executive compensation.

Data Source and Methodology

For the firm performance data, we have used the *COMPUSTAT* annual data files for both 1989 and 1999. The following data were obtained from *COMPUSTAT*: debt/asset ratios, asset size, 3-year average of the growth rate of sales, net income, and 1-year stock price return of firms. We have also divided the firms into manufacturing and service companies and used the dummy variables to capture the industry characteristics. After carefully matching firm data with executive compensation, we have selected 336 surviving firms for both 1989 and 1999 time periods.

As for the executive compensation data of major U.S. firms, we have used the *Forbes* magazine's list of the 500 largest U.S. firms as measured by sales, total assets, market value of equity or profits. For each firm, we obtain the data on the CEO's annual salary and bonus (SB), as well as the annual total compensation (TComp) from *Forbes*' annual survey of top executive compensation, covering both 1989 and 1999. Total compensation equals salary and bonus, plus payments made under long-term compensation plans, restricted stock awards vested or released from restrictions during the year, thrift plan contributions, and other benefits. Ideally, it should also include the *ex-ante* value of stock options granted during the year, but unfortunately, *Forbes* does not report this data. However, Yermack has found that the median value of stock options granted is under 10 percent of a CEO's total compensation. Therefore, its omission should not cause a significant bias.

We have fitted the OLS regression models to the data to calculate the association among the dependent and independent variables as prescribed by our hypothesis. Our models in general are:

SB	=	Salary and bonus of the CEO
Tcomp	=	Total compensation of the CEO
Xo	=	Intercept

DA	=	Total debts/total assets
FS	=	Firm size
GR	=	3-year average growth rate of sales
NI	=	Net income
SPR	=	Stock price return (1-year)
DV	=	Dummy variables.

Following our null hypothesis, we will expect all the independent variables to be positively and significantly associated with executive compensation, taking both salary and bonus (SB) and total compensation (TComp) of the CEOs into account. The dummy variables will be used, assigning 0 for the manufacturing firms and 1 for the service firms, to examine whether they have any significant effect on executive compensation. Here also, we will expect positive and significant association of the dummy variables with the executive compensation during the period covered by our study.

Empirical Results

In table 7.1, we have shown the regression results of capital structure and executive compensation for 1999 with salary and bonus (SB) of the CEO as the dependent variable. Here we find that the β-coefficient for the capital structure variable (i.e., total debts/ total assets) was highly significant, explaining over 14 percent variation in executive compensation with capital structure during 1999. Similarly, the 3-year average

Table 7.1
Capital Structure and Executive Compensation - 1999
(SB as the Dependant Variable)

Independent Variable	Intercept	β-Coefficients	t-values
	X_0=11.3216		4.5181***
X1		0.148272	2.344186**
X2		0.001376	11.069428***
X3		0.153185	2.558458**
X4		0.025133	0.198048
X5		0.063730	3.413130***
N=336			
R2=.2956			
F Ratio = 14.7387			

* Significant at the 10% level
** Significant at the 5% level
***Significant at the 1% level

sales growth rate was also very significant, explaining over 15 percent with the executive compensation. The variable representing 1-year stock price return was also significant, associating with 6 percent variation in executive compensation. The β-coefficient of firm size as an explanatory variable was extremely small although statistically highly significant, while the β-coefficient of the NI variable, although associated with 2 percent variation in executive compensation, was not statistically significant at all in 1999.

When we use the same regression equation for 1989, as shown in table 7.2, we find that here also, the capital structure variable was strongly associated with executive compensation (SB), explaining over 5 percent variation in executive compensation and being statistically significant at the 5 percent level. Next came the stock price return variable which explained over 3 percent variation with the executive compensation, being statistically significant at the 1 percent level. But the firm size variable, although statistically highly significant, "explained" very little of the variation with capital structure, while both the sales growth and net income as independent variables were not statistically significant at all in 1989.

In table 7.3, we have shown the relationship between capital structure and executive compensation for 1999, where the latter includes stock options, beside salary and bonus of the selected firms. Here again, the capital structure variable was significantly associated with the total

Table 7.2
Capital Structure and Executive Compensation – 1989
(SB as the Dependant Variable)

Independent Variables	Intercept	B-Coefficients	t-values
	X0=63.2439	6.5639***	
X1		0.055567	2.410748**
X2		0.000908	4.624653***
X3		0.001636	0.731116
X4		0.059229	0.867923
X5		0.036243	3.036584***
N=336			
R2=.233352			
F Ratio = 12.4377			

* Significant at the 10% level
** Significant at the 5% level
***Significant at the 1% level

Table 7.3
Capital Structure and Executive Compensation - 1989
(TComp as the Dependant Variable)

Independent Variables	Intercept	β-Coefficients	t-values
	X0=76.1718		10.5748***
X1		0.051926	2.286889**
X2		0.009202	4.688809***
X3		0.001613	1.976631
X4		0.029886	0.447163
X5		0.038902	3.255291***
N = 336			
R2 = .1119			
F Ratio = 8.2921			

* Significant at the 10% level
** Significant at the 5% level
***Significant at the 1% level

compensation of the CEO of the firms, although not as strongly as the salary and bonus components of the CEOs. The β-coefficients of both the sales growth rate and the stock price return as independent variables were highly significant and they both jointly "explained" over 20 percent of the variation with executive compensation. But both firm size and net income as independent variables were not statistically significant at all in 1999.

When we use Tcomp as the dependent variable for 1989, as shown in table 7.4, the capital structure variable was again statistically significant, although the b-value was slightly less as compared to 1999. But beside this variable, only the stock price return was statistically significant for this year. It is interesting to note that the sales growth variable, which was highly significant in 1999, was not statistically significant at all in 1989. The net income variable was not statistically significant for both 1989 and 1999.

In table 7.5, we have taken industry classification as the dummy variable to capture any industry characteristic as an "explanatory" variable. Here we have incorporated salary and bonus, as well as total compensation of the CEOs for 1999. Here also, capital structure variable was significantly associated with both salary and bonus, as well as the total compensation of the CEOs. Net income was not statistically significant with salary and bonus, but was statistically significant for total compensation as the dependent variable. It is interesting to note that firm size

Table 7.4
Capital Structure and Executive Compensation – 1989
(TComp as the Dependent Variable)

Independent Variables	Intercept	β-Coefficients	t-values
	X0=76.1718		10.5748***
X1		0.051926	2.286889**
X2		0.009202	4.688809***
X3		0.001613	1.976631
X4		0.029886	0.447163
X5		0.038902	3.255291***
N = 336			
R2 = .1119			
F Ratio = 8.2921			

* Significant at the 10% level
** Significant at the 5% level
***Significant at the 1% level

Table 7.5
Capital Structure and Executive Compensation – 1999
(With Dummy Variables)

Independent Variables	SB as Dependent Variable		TComp as a dep. Variable	
	β-coefficient	t-values	β-coefficient	t-values
X1	0.0639	4.4010***	0.0593	2.9755**
X2	0.0011	5.0921***	0.0015	2.8644**
X3	0.0248	1.5318*	0.0145	0.4184
X4	0.0501	0.2671	0.0237	1.9375*
X5	0.0315	2.5187**	0.0472	2.2009**
X6	-2.7621	-0.6091	-1.0224	-0.7143
N=336				
R2	0.4712	0.2683		
F ratio	13.2186	5.5616		

* Significant at the 10% level
** Significant at the 5% level
***Significant at the 1% level

came out to be statistically significant although it "explained" very little of the variation of the dependent variable in the equations. Similarly stock price return was highly significant in both the equations as they explained over 3 percent and 4 percent variation, with salary and bonus, and total compensation, respectively, for the year 1999. But the dummy variables, taking industry characteristics as manufacturing or service industry, were not significant at all in 1999.

Concluding Remarks

Our study thus finds a positive and statistically significant association between the salary and bonuses of the chief executives of the largest U.S. corporations taken in our sample and the debt/asset ratios of these companies during 1987-1999. This was also true for the case of of total compensation of the CEOs. The regression analyses also show a positive association between executive compensation and sales growth as well as between executive compensation and stock price return, but no relation with net income and firm size. It seems that the risk-return relationship is also valid for the executive compensation of the largest firms in the United States.

References

Agrawal, A., and G. N. Mandelker, "Managerial Incentives and Corporate Investment and Financing Decisions," *Journal of Finance*, September 1987.

Agrawal, A. and C. R. Knoeber, "Managerial Compensation and the Threat of Takeover," *Journal of Finance*, June 1998.

Baker, G., M. C. Jensen, and K. L. Murphy, "Compensation and Incentives: Theory vs. Practice," *Journal of Finance*, July 1988.

Fisher, A., "Readers on CEO Pay: Many are Angry, a Few Really Think the Big Guy is Worth it," *Fortune*, 1998.

Ghosh, Arvin and Francis Cai "The Determinants of Capital Structure," *American Business Review*, June 2000.

Mehran, H., "Executive Compensation Structure, Ownership, and Firm Performance," *Journal of Financial Economics*, 1995, 163-184.

Simarly, R. L., Minfang Li, and K. E. Bass, "CEO Compensation and Corporate Social Performance," Working Paper, 2000.

Titman, S., and R. Wessels, "The Determinants of Capital Structure Choice," *Journal of Finance*, 1988, 1-19.

8

Debt Financing and Ownership Structure

Agency theorists have long recognized that the separation of ownership and control common in most corporations creates conflicts of interest between a firm's managers and shareholders. These conflicts (agency problems) arise because managers have the opportunity to use the assets of the firm in ways that benefit themselves personally but decrease the wealth of the firm's shareholders. Examples of this type of opportunistic behavior by managers include consuming an excessive amount of perks, shirking their responsibilities, and investing in negative net present value (NPV) projects that offer personal diversification benefits to the firm's managers. Amihud and Lev (1981) and Friend and Hasbrouck (1988) believe that some of this opportunistic behavior results because many managers have large proportions of their personal wealth invested in their firm's common stock and in firm-specific human capital. Because their personal wealth is heavily invested in their employers, these managers will lose a large part of their personal wealth if their employer goes bankrupt. Risk-averse managers may seek to mitigate this risk by acting to reduce the bankruptcy risk of the firm. Friend and Hasbrouck (1988) suggest that one way to accomplish this is to use less than the optimal amount of debt in the firm's capital structure. Further, the authors argue that the greater the proportion of personal wealth that managers have tied up in the firm's common stock and firm-specific human capital the greater their incentive to minimize the use of debt in the firm's capital structure.

Friend and Lang (1988) and Berger, Ofek, and Yermack (1997) tested to see if there is a relationship between managerial wealth invested in the firm and the amount of debt in the firm's capital structure. Friend and Lang (1988) used as their measures of managerial wealth invested in the firm the proportion of the firm's common stock owned by the firm's largest insider and the market value of the largest insider's stock holdings.

They found an inverse relationship between both of these variables and the amount of debt in the firm's capital structure. However, the market value of the insider's shares was found to be more strongly correlated with the amount of debt in the firm's capital structure. Friend and Lang also found that the presence of a blockholder, one who owned at least 10 percent of the firm's common stock, was associated with higher levels of debt financing by the firm. Berger, Ofek, and Yermack (1997) also found that the presence of a blockholder (5 percent) is associated with higher levels of debt financing. Berger et al. also found that the percentage of a firm's shares owned by the CEO is directly related to the amount of debt in a firm's capital structure. This is in conflict with results reported by Friend and Lang.

In this study, we seek to expand on the previous research by seeking to resolve the conflict over the relationship between managerial share ownership and firm debt financing and to determine if this relationship is different for firms listed on the New York Stock Exchange (NYSE) and those listed on the NASDAQ stock market. Previous studies have mostly used NYSE firms in their analysis and those that have included NASDAQ firms have not tested for differences between the two groups of firms. For this study, we have obtained a sample of NYSE and NASDAQ firms and gathered share ownership and capital structure data for each group of firms for the year 2000 and for NYSE firms for 1993. Our results indicate that NASDAQ firms use less debt in their capital structures and have higher share ownership by managers and blockholders than NYSE firms. We also found that NYSE firms decreased the amount of debt in their capital structures and showed an increase in blockholder share ownership between 1993 and 2000. Further, NYSE firms were found to exhibit an inverse (direct) relationship between managerial (blockholder) share ownership and the amount of debt in their capital structures. For NASDAQ firms, a direct relationship was also found between blockholder share ownership and the amount of debt in their capital structures. Debt structure was found to be unrelated to managerial share ownership for NASDAQ firms.

Debt Financing and its Determinants

Most firms use some debt in their capital structure. The primary reason for doing so is that the tax deductibility of interest lowers the cost of debt financing and makes debt capital the cheapest type of outside financing available to most firms. The major disadvantage of debt financing is that it increases the risk that the firm will go bankrupt if it can not service its debt. This bankruptcy risk is not particularly worrisome for an investor who holds a well-diversified portfolio of investments because the bankruptcy of any one firm in their portfolio of investments will not have a large impact on their wealth. Consequently, a well-diversified investor will prefer that most firms use significant amounts of debt capital in their capital structures. Amihud and Lev (1981) and Friend and Hasbrouck (1988) believe managerial insiders (officers and directors) have a somewhat different perspective since many of them have large portions of their personal wealth invested in their employers. The personal wealth a managerial insider has invested in their employer is composed largely of their employer's common stock and the firm-specific human capital they have accumulated while working for their employer. Because these items tend to represent a large proportion of an insider's total wealth, the bankruptcy of their employer would have a major impact on their personal wealth. As a result, Friend and Hasbrouck (1988) argue that managerial insiders should be much more sensitive to the bankruptcy risk debt financing induces than the typical shareholder and may be inclined to minimize this risk by using less than the optimal (shareholder wealth maximizing) amount of debt in the firm's capital structure. Further, the more wealth a managerial insider has invested in their employer the greater the incentive they have to minimize the use of debt financing.

The shareholders' problem is to make certain that managerial insiders do not succumb to their own personal financial incentives and use less than the optimal amount of debt in the firm's capital structure. In this study, we seek to ascertain if an inverse relationship does exist between managerial share ownership and the amount of debt in a firm's capital structure. We also seek to determine if, as suggested by Shleifer and Vishny (1986), blockholder share ownership can mitigate this agency problem and if NASDAQ firms are different in these regards than NYSE firms. Shareholders of a corporation have a residual claim on the earnings and assets of the firm and therefore, bear proportional to their share ownership, the economic consequences of actions taken by the firm's managers and directors. If managerial insiders engage in opportunistic behavior, shareholders bear a pro rata share of the costs of such actions. Consequently, a shareholder's incentive to monitor insiders and make certain the firm is being properly managed is directly related to the proportion of the firm's shares that the shareholder owns. This implies that a particular type of shareholder, blockholders (those who own at least 5 percent of a firm's common stock), have a strong incentive to seek to control the opportunistic behavior of the firm's managerial insiders.

Consequently, greater blockholder share ownership in a firm should lead to greater monitoring of the firm by blockholders and result in more debt financing being used by the firm than its managerial insiders desire.

As NASDAQ firms tend to be newer, smaller, and riskier than NYSE firms, these characteristics may affect the relationships between managerial and blockholder share ownership and firm capital structure. Additionally, the higher risk and the lack of an extended credit history that these firms have should also limit the ability of NASDAQ firms to borrow and cause them to have less debt in their capital structures than NYSE firms.

Empirical Results

To test the above theories a sample of ninety-nine NYSE firms and ninety-two NASDAQ firms was selected. The SEC's Edgar database was used to obtain ownership and debt structure data for the sample firms for 2000 from the firm's proxy and 10-K forms. Similar data was obtained for the NYSE firms for 1993 as well. This could not be done for the NASDAQ firms as a large number of those firms did not have forms on file with the SEC covering the 1993 fiscal year. The dearth of filings undoubtedly occurred because many of the NASDAQ firms either did not exist or did not have publicly traded common stock in 1993.

Summary statistics for selected variables for the NYSE and NASDAQ firms in 2000 are contained in table 8.1. Predictably, the NYSE firms in the sample are much larger than the NASDAQ firms. The NYSE firms have mean total assets of $66.6 billion while NASDAQ firms have average total assets of $5.16 billion. As expected, NYSE firms also use more debt in their capital structures than NASDAQ firms. The NYSE firms

Table 8.1
Means of Selected Variables for NYSE and NASDAQ Firms in 2000

	NYSE		NASDAQ	
	Mean	Median	Mean	Median
Total Assets ($B)	66.6	24.9	5.16	1.99
Debt ($B)	18.9	5.95	.632	.054
Managers (M shares)	10.5	2.30	46.0	6.58
Blockholder (M shares)	79.1	38.1	75.4	28.7
Debt Ratio (%)	26.6	25.2	11.7	2.86
Managers (%)	1.96	.493	6.67	2.66
Blockholders (%)	15.4	12.4	21.5	20.1

B = billion
M = million

have, on average, \$18.9 billion in total debt as compared to \$.632 billion for NASDAQ firms. When total debt is expressed as a percentage of total assets (Debt Ratio), similar results are found. The mean Debt Ratio for NYSE firms is 26.6 percent versus 11.7 percent for NASDAQ firms. The difference in debt ratios of 14.9 percent is significant at the 1 percent level (z = 5.90). Additionally, managerial share ownership is higher in NASDAQ firms (46.0 million shares) than it is in NYSE firms (10.5 million shares). Expressed as a percentage of shares outstanding (Managers (%)), the mean value of managerial share ownership for NASDAQ firms (6.67 percent) is also higher than the corresponding figure for NYSE firms (1.96 percent). The difference in mean share ownership of 4.71 percent is statistically significant at the 1 percent level (z = 4.27). The number of shares owned by blockholders is similar for NYSE and NASDAQ firms (79.1 million shares versus 75.4 million shares). When blockholder share ownership is expressed as a percentage of shares outstanding (Blockholders (%)), a different result emerges. The mean value of Blockholders (%) for NASDAQ firms is 21.5 percent as compared to 15.4 percent for NYSE firms. The difference in mean blockholder share ownership of 6.1 percent is significant at the 5 percent level (z = 2.55). In sum, NYSE firms are larger, have more debt in their capital structures, and have a smaller percentage of their shares owned by managers and blockholders than NASDAQ firms.

Table 8.2 contains summary statistics for selected variables for the NYSE firms in 1993 and 2000. Scanning table 8.2 reveals that their have been some changes in the capital and ownership structures of the NYSE firms between 1993 and 2000. For example, average total assets of the NYSE firms increased by 185 percent over the period from \$23.4 billion in 1993 to \$66.6 billion in 2000. The mean total debt of the firms increased from \$8.27 billion to \$18.9 billion, an increase of 129 percent. Nevertheless, the average Debt Ratio of the NYSE firms actually decreased over the period from 29.2 percent to 26.6 percent. The decline in the Debt Ratio of 2.6 percent is significant at the 10 percent level. Thus, even though the dollar amount of debt in the firm's capital structure increased markedly over the period, mean total assets grew even faster. Interestingly, the mean share ownership of the firm managers stayed relatively constant over the period at just over 10 million shares. The average percentage of the firm's shares owned by managers dropped from 3.30 percent to 1.96 percent, however, the change is not statistically significant. Blockholder share ownership, on the other hand, increased from an average of 27.0 million shares in 1993 to 79.1 million in 2000.

Table 8.2
Means of Selected Variables for NYSE Firms in 1993 and 2000

	1993		2000	
	Mean	Median	Mean	Median
Total Assets ($B)	23.4	10.7	66.6	24.9
Debt ($B)	8.27	3.36	18.9	5.95
Managers (M shares)	10.1	.614	10.5	2.30
Blockholder (M shares)	27.0	6.12	79.1	38.1
Debt Ratio (%)	29.2	27.7	26.6	25.2
Managers (%)	3.30	.405	1.96	.493
Blockholders (%)	10.8	4.74	15.4	12.4

B = billion
M = million

This corresponds to a 193 percent increase in blockholder share ownership. As a percentage of shares outstanding, blockholder share ownership increased from 10.8 percent in 1993 to 15.4 percent in 2000. This 4.6 percent increase in blockholder share ownership is significant at the 5 percent level (z = 2.26). Overall, from 1993 to 2000, the NYSE sample firms grew at a very high rate and experienced significant decreases in the percentage of debt in their capital structures and significant increases in blockholder share ownership.

Next, a univariate analysis is used to test for the relationship between managerial and blockholder share ownership and the amount of debt in a firm's capital structure. First, the NASDAQ firms are ranked (using data from 2000) by managerial share ownership, divided into three subgroups, and the mean Debt Ratio is calculated for each subgroup. The results are presented in the first two columns of table 8.3. As expected, firms with the highest level of managerial share ownership have the smallest mean Debt Ratio (13.8 percent) and firms with the lowest managerial share ownership have the highest mean Debt Ratio (14.0 percent). However, the difference in mean Debt Ratios is small (-0.2%) and not statistically significant. The last two columns of table 8.3 contain a similar analysis in which firms are ranked and grouped by blockholder share ownership.

As predicted, the firms with the highest level of blockholder share ownership have the highest mean Debt Ratio (15.1 percent) and firms with the lowest blockholder share ownership have the lowest mean Debt Ratio (11.0 percent). The difference in mean Debt Ratios is not statistically significant. Table 8.4 contains a similar analysis performed on NYSE firms using data from 2000. Contrary to expectations, NYSE firms with the highest (lowest) managerial share ownership have the highest

Table 8.3
Univariate Analysis of NASDAQ Firms' Debt Structure in 2000

Manager Share Own.	Debt Ratio	Blockholder Share Own.	Debt Ratio
Low	14.0	Low	11.0
Med	7.3	Med	9.1
High	13.8	High	15.1
High-Low	-0.2	High-Low	4.1
(Z value)	(-0.04)		(0.81)

a = significant at the 10% level
b = significant at the 5% level
c = significant at the 1% level

Table 8.4
Univariate Analysis of NYSE Firms' Debt Structure in 2000

Manager Share Own.	Debt Ratio	Blockholder Share Own.	Debt Ratio
Low	21.7	Low	21.4
Med	28.9	Med	25.9
High	29.3	High	32.7
High-Low	7.6[a]	High-Low	11.3[b]
(Z value)	(1.76)		(2.59)

a = significant at the 10% level
b = significant at the 5% level
c = significant at the 1% level

(lowest) mean Debt Ratio. The difference in mean Debt Ratios of 7.6 percent is significant at the 10 percent level. When the NYSE firms are ranked and grouped by blockholder share ownership, the highest (lowest) blockholder share ownership subgroup is found to have the highest (lowest) mean Debt Ratio. The difference in mean Debt Ratios of 11.3 percent is significant at the 5 percent level. The analysis is repeated on the NYSE firms using data from 1993 and the results are presented in table 8.5. With the 1993 data, the highest mean debt ratio occurs in the subgroups of firms with the lowest managerial and blockholder share ownership. However, no statistically significant difference between the high and low share ownership subgroups mean Debt Ratios was found. In sum, the results of the univariate analysis are generally (but not entirely) consistent with agency theory predictions.

Finally, a regression analysis is used to test for the effects of managerial and blockholder share ownership on the amount of debt in a firm's capital structure. The results of this regression analysis are contained in table 8.6. In each of the regressions, the dependent variable employed

Table 8.5
Univariate Analysis of NYSE Firms' Debt Structure in 1993

Manager Share Own	Debt Ratio	Blockholder Share Own	Debt Ratio
Low	30.0	Low	30.4
Med	28.9	Med	29.8
High	28.8	High	27.4
High-Low	-1.2	High-Low	-3.0
(Z value)	(-0.29)		(-0.70)

a = significant at the 10% level
b = significant at the 5% level
c = significant at the 1% level

Table 8.6
Regression Analysis of Debt Structure Determinants

Dependent Variable	Debt Ratio	Debt Ratio
Intercept	25.3[c]	26.0[c]
(Z value)	(15.7)	(15.2)
Total Assets ($B)	.019	.017
	(1.34)	(1.22)
NASDAQ	-16.2[c]	-19.0[c]
	(-7.19)	(-5.67)
Managers (%)	-.167	-.379[b]
	(-1.30)	(-2.30)
Blockholders (%)	.168[b]	.166[b]
	(2.55)	(2.13)
Managers NASDAQ	-	.523[b]
	(1.97)	
Blockholders NASDAQ	-	.005
	(0.04)	
Adj. R^2	17.7	18.5
F value	16.5	11.9
N	290	290

B = billion

a = significant at the 10% level
b = significant at the 5% level
c = significant at the 1% level

is the firm's Debt Ratio and the analysis was performed using the combined data from the NYSE firms in 1993 and 2000 and from the NASDAQ firms in 2000. Two control variables, total assets and a NASDAQ dummy variable, are used in the regressions. Total assets is used as a control variable because larger firms are thought to have better access to the credit markets and, therefore, should tend to have more debt in their capital structures than smaller firms. The dummy variable (NASDAQ) takes on a value of one if the firm is listed on the NASDAQ stock market and zero if it is listed on the NYSE. This variable is used to control for the difference in the average debt ratio for NYSE and NASDAQ firms discussed previously. In both regressions, the coefficient on Total Assets is positive but not statistically significant. The coefficients on NASDAQ are both negative and significant at the 1 percent level. The -16.2 (-19.0) coefficient in the first (second) regression indicates that after adjusting for size and ownership structure effects, NASDAQ firms have, on average, a debt ratio that is 16.2 percent (19.0 percent) less than the debt ratio of NYSE firms. In the first regression, no attempt is made to differentiate between the ownership structure effects on capital structure for NYSE and NASDAQ firms. Consequently, the coefficients on Managers and Blockholders represent the average affect of these variables on a firm's debt ratio across NYSE and NASDAQ firms. As predicted, the coefficient on Managers is negative, but not statistically significant. The coefficient on Blockholders is positive, as expected, and significant at the 5 percent level. The previous two results suggest that the amount of debt financing a firm uses is inversely related to managerial share ownership and directly related to blockholder share ownership.

In the second regression, we seek to ascertain if there is any difference in the relationship between the ownership structure variables and firm debt financing for NYSE and NASDAQ firms. To accomplish this, two interactive variables are added to the set of independent variables used in the regression. The first is the NASDAQ dummy variable (NASDAQ) multiplied by the percentage of managerial share ownership (Managers). The second is the NASDAQ dummy multiplied by the percentage of Blockholder share ownership. In the second regression, the coefficients on the independent variables Managers and Blockholders captures the relationship between the firm's ownership structure and the amount of debt in its capital structure for NYSE firms only. The coefficient on Managers is negative and significant at the 5 percent level while the coefficient on Blockholders is positive and significant at the 5 percent level. Thus, for NYSE firms, the predicted relationships between the ownership structure variables and the percentage of debt in the firm's capital structure are confirmed. For NASDAQ firms, the coefficient on the Managers NASDAQ interactive variable captures the differential impact of managerial share ownership on the firm's capital structure. Since the coefficient on this interactive variable is significant at the 5 percent level, this indicates that the relationship between managerial share ownership and the amount of debt in the firm's capital structure is different for NASDAQ firms. The managerial share ownership effect on capital structure for NASDAQ firms is captured by summing the coefficients on Managers and the Managers NASDAQ interactive variable. The sum of those coefficients, .144 (-.379 + .523), is not statistically significant. This indicates that for NASDAQ firms, there is no relationship between managerial share ownership and the amount of debt financing the firm employs. The interactive variable Blockholders NASDAQ captures the differential impact of blockholder share ownership on firm capital structure for NASDAQ firms. As the coefficient on this variable is statistically insignificant, this indicates that the relationship between blockholder share ownership and the amount of debt in the firm's capital structure is the same for both NYSE and NASDAQ firms.

Concluding Remarks

We have thus seen that there is an inverse relationship between the managerial ownership of stocks and the capital structure of firms belonging to the NYSE, but not for firms in the NASDAQ market. But there is a positive relationship between the blockholder ownership of stocks and capital structure for both NYSE and NASDAQ firms. We have also found that the NASDAQ firms have lower debt ratios and higher managerial and blockholder ownership of stocks as compared to the NYSE firms.

References

Amihud, Y. and B. Lev. (1981), "Risk Reduction as a Managerial Motive for Conglomerate Mergers," *Bell Journal of Economics*, Vol. 12, No. 2, pp. 605-17.

Berger, P., E. Ofek, and D. Yermack, (1997), "Managerial Entrenchment and Capital Structure Decisions," *Journal of Finance*, Vol. 52, No. 4, pp. 1411-38.

Fama, E. and M. Jensen, (1983), "Separation of Ownership and Control," *Journal of Law and Economics*, Vol. 26, No. 2, pp. 301-325.

Friend, I. and J. Hasbrouck, (1988), "Determinants of Capital Structure," *Research in Finance*, Vol. 7, No. 1, pp. 1-19.

Friend, I. and L. Lang, (1988), "An Empirical Test of the Impact of Managerial Self-Interest on Corporate Capital Structure," *Journal of Finance*, Vol. 43, No. 2, pp. 271-81.

Shleifer, A. and R. Vishny, (1986), "Large Shareholders and Corporate Control," *Journal of Political Economy*, Vol. 94, No. 3, pp. 461-88.

9

Capital Structure and Firm Profitability: NYSE and NASDAQ Firms

Recently, Fama and French (2001) showed that over the last twenty or so years a large number of companies have stopped paying dividends to their common stockholders. Specifically, in 1978, 66.5 percent of publicly-traded firms paid dividends but by 1999 only 20.8 percent of firms paid dividends. Part of the reason for this decline in the percentage of firms paying dividends occurred because of a shift in the characteristics of the universe of publicly-traded firms. Today, there are many more small, unprofitable, high-growth firms than there were in the past. However, a large part of the reduction in the percentage of dividend-paying firms can not be explained in terms of shifts in firm characteristics. Fama and French conclude this means that there has also been a general reduction in the propensity of firms to pay dividends. One possible explanation for this reduction in the percentage of dividend paying firms is that firms have decided to rely more on internally-generated funds to finance their investment opportunities than they have in the past. By not raising capital in the public financial markets, firms avoid the flotation costs, information disclosure, information asymmetry, and delays in raising capital associated with the public offering of securities. Formally, this is the "pecking order theory" of firm capital structure suggested by Myers (1984) and Myers and Majluf (1984). Assuming the "pecking order theory" is the correct explanation of the dividend reductions firms will, among other things, also be using less debt capital to finance their investments than they have in the past. The net result of this is that there should be a noticeable decrease in the amount of debt in the average firm's capital over the last twenty years.

In this study, we seek to ascertain if there actually has been a decrease in the amount of debt in the typical firm's capital structure over the last twenty years. Further, we seek to determine if the change in capital structure is different for NYSE and NASDAQ firms. It is generally thought that because NASDAQ firms are smaller, newer, less profitable, and riskier than NYSE firms they have had limited access to the credit markets and therefore have generally used less debt in their capital structures than NYSE firms. If this is true, NASDAQ firms should also have been less able to shift their capital structures toward more internal and less debt financing. Additionally, we will test to see if the relationship between firm profitability and the amount of debt in the typical firm's capital structure is different for NYSE and NASDAQ firms.

Data and Sample Selection

Our base sample is all firms listed on the NYSE and NASDAQ stock markets that are reported on the *COMPUSTAT* database (10-29-04 version). Firms in the utilities and financial services industries were eliminated from the base sample because of the potential biases associated with the heavy regulation of those industries. Companies with negative net worths in any sample year were also eliminated from the base sample because of the distorted capital structures of these firms. Outliers, firms with return on assets of more than 100 percent or less than -100 percent, were also eliminated from the base sample. This resulted in a final sample of 1,022 NYSE and 1,772 NASDAQ firms. Data for each sample company for the sample years 1985, 1989, 1994, 1999, and 2003 was obtained from *COMPUSTAT*. Some companies did not have data for every sample year. Previous studies such as Friend and Lang (1988) and Berger, Ofek, and Yermack (1997) have shown that the amount of debt in a firm's capital structure is affected by a number of factors including primarily firm size, risk, collateral availability, and growth opportunities. We will control for all of these factors in our analysis. Our firm size proxies are total assets (Assets), sales (Sales), and the market value of common equity (MVE). Collateral availability is measured by the firm's net property, plant, and equipment to total assets ratio (PPE). Growth opportunities are measured by the market to book value of common equity (MVE/BE) and Tobin's q. Tobin's q is calculated as the sum of the book values of debt and preferred equity plus the market value of common equity divided by the sum of the book values of debt, preferred, and common equity.

There are two well-known theories that seek to explain the relationship between profitability and the amount of debt in a firm's capital structure. Jensen (1986) believes that greater profitability should result in more debt usage by firms in order to control the agency costs associated with free cash flow. Specifically, the increased debt service requirements caused by additional debt will force managers to pay out more of the firm's free cash flows to creditors and leave less money for managers to use for things that do not benefit the firm's shareholders. Jensen's theory implies a direct relationship, profitability and the amount of debt in a firm's capital structure. Myers and Majluf (1984), however, argue that if there is asymmetric information in the capital markets, new security issues (debt and equity) will be undervalued by investors and the firm will be better off financing its investments with internally-generated funds. Firms will, therefore, only finance with outside debt capital when internally-generated funds are insufficient to fully fund the firm's investment opportunities. Myers and Majluf's theory implies an inverse relationship between profitability and the amount of debt in the firm's capital structure. Our empirical analysis should indicate which of these two theories is correct. Additionally, we will test to see if the relationship between firm profitability and the amount of debt in the typical firm's capital structure has changed over the last twenty years. Profitability is measured by sample year return on assets (ROA), return on equity (ROE), and operating cash flow divided by total assets (CF/Assets). Firm risk is measured by the standard deviation of ROA, ROE, and CF/Assets over the five-year period from sample year t to year t – 4.

Empirical Results

The mean values of selected variables for the NASDAQ sample firms for each of the sample years are presented in table 9.1. Looking first at the size proxies, it is evident that the average size of NASDAQ firms has grown considerably over the sample period. For example, mean Assets grew from $359 million in 1985 to $722 million in 2003. As for capital structure, there is a noticeable decrease in the amount of debt in the sample firms' capital structures. The mean total debt to total assets ratio (Debt/Assets) declined from .204 in 1985 to .141 in 2003. Similarly, the mean total debt to total capital ratio (Debt/T. Cap.) dropped from .275 in 1985 to .188 in 2003. Total capital is the sum of the book values of debt, preferred, and common equity. Interestingly, firm profitability has also decreased over the sample period. Mean ROA for the sample firms dropped from .018 (1.8 percent) in 1985 to -.024 in 2003. Similar decreases in ROE and CF/Assets are also evident. The data shows that NASDAQ firms' growth opportunities have grown over time as both mean MVE/BE and Tobin's q have increased over the sample period. Mean PPE declined from .304 in 1985 to .211 in 2003, indicating that NASDAQ firms have significantly less collateral available to pledge on debt than they used to.

NYSE firms display many, but not all, of the trends exhibited by NASDAQ firms (see table 9.2). For example, mean Assets grew substantially over the sample period from $2.463 billion in 1985 to $8.678 billion in 2003. Also, comparing mean Assets figures, it is evident that the average NYSE firm is approximately ten times larger than the average NASDAQ firm. The mean profitability of the NYSE firms has also declined over the sample period. For example, mean ROA declined from .060 (6.0 percent) in 1985 to .042 in 2003. Other profitability measures exhibit a similar trend. Growth opportunities for NYSE firms have also increased as indicated by the increase in MVE/BE from 2.18 in 1985 to 2.69 in 2003. There has also been a slight decline in collateral availability (PPE) in recent years. The one trend that is different for NYSE firms relates to their capital structures. Examining the Debt/Assets ratio, the noticeable decrease in the amount of debt in NASDAQ firms' capital structures is not evident for NYSE firms. In fact, there is no discernible trend in the capital structures of NYSE firms. However, the typical NYSE firm has,

Table 9.1
Summary Statistics for Selected Variables for the NASDAQ Firms

Panel A: Firm Size					
	1985	1989	1994	1999	2003
Assets ($M)	359	606	600	581	722
Sales ($M)	644	788	753	631	708
MVE ($M)	195	396	494	1779	1194
Panel B: Capital Structure					
Debt ($M)	123	219	207	148	158
Debt/Assets	.204	.209	.156	.155	.141
Debt/T. Cap.	.275	.276	.210	.200	.188
Panel C: Profitability, Growth, etc.					
ROA	.018	.023	.020	-.009	-.024
ROE	.048	.041	.051	-.003	-.038
CF/Assets	.106	.102	.099	.062	.049
MVE/BE	2.71	2.58	2.69	5.52	3.64
Tobin's q	2.31	2.15	2.44	5.01	3.08
PPE	.304	.286	.260	.230	.211

M = million

on average, more debt in its capital structure in each sample year than the average NASDAQ firm (8 percent to 10 percent more over the last decade).

Our next objective is to test for the relationship, if any, between firm profitability and capital structure and to see if this relationship has changed over time. This will be accomplished with a regression analysis in which the firm's Debt/Assets ratio is used as the dependent variable. A separate regression will be run for each sample year. In each regression, control variables for firm size, collateral, growth opportunities, and risk will be employed. The main independent variables of interest are profitability measures (ROA and Average ROA). ROA measures current year profitability while Average ROA (average annual ROA over years t to t - 4) measures long-term profitability. In table 9.3, the results of the regressions for NASDAQ firms are presented. In these regressions, firm size (Assets) is highly correlated with the amount of debt in the sample firms' capital structures. In each of the sample year regressions, the coefficient of Assets is positive and significant at the 1 percent level. Collateral availability is also shown to be a significant determinant of firm capital structure. The coefficients of PPE are all positive and significant at the 1 percent level. The coefficients of Tobin's q are all negative and significant at the 5 percent level or better in each regression. This indicates that high growth firms tend to use less debt in their capital structures than low growth firms. Firm risk is also seen to be an important determinant of firm capital structure as indicated by the coefficients of Std. ROA. These coefficients are all negative and three are significant at the 10 percent level or better. This result indicates that high risk firms tend to use less debt in their capital structures than low risk firms. The relationship between firm profitability and capital structure is much weaker. Looking at current year's profitability (ROA), only one coefficient is statistically significant at conventional levels and the sign of that coefficient is positive. For long-term profitability (Avg. ROA), the coefficients are all negative, but only one is significant at the 5 percent level or better. In sum, these results indicate there is little or no relationship between firm profitability and the amount of debt in NASDAQ firms' capital structures.

Other dependent and control variables were also tried in the above regressions. Sales and MVE were tried as size proxies but did not improve on the above results. ROE and CF/Assets were also used as profitability measures but were generally not as strongly correlated with firm capital structure as ROA. MVE/BE was also employed as a growth proxy with results similar to those reported above. Debt/T. Cap. was substituted as the

Table 9.2
Summary Statistics for Selected Variables for the NYSE Firms

	1985	1989	1994	1999	2003
Panel A: Firm Size					
Assets ($M)	2463	4075	4767	6247	8678
Sales ($M)	2830	3759	4297	5450	7163
MVE ($M)	1868	2808	3508	9074	8416
Panel B: Capital Structure					
Debt ($M)	536	1355	1399	1929	2571
Debt/Assets	.215	.251	.230	.269	.239
Debt/T. Cap.	.296	.346	.327	.373	.344
Panel C: Profitability, Growth, etc.					
ROA	.060	.062	.062	.054	.042
ROE	.115	.128	.131	.127	.092
CF/Assets	.164	.160	.161	.153	.133
MVE/BE	2.18	2.30	2.55	3.16	2.69
Tobin's q	1.88	1.89	2.08	2.42	2.08
PPE	.368	.368	.374	.356	.338

M = million

capital structure proxy with little effect. In sum, none of these variables improved on the results presented above.

Table 9.4 contains the results of a similar regression analysis performed on NYSE firms. The coefficients of the four control variables in the NYSE regressions are similar to those of the corresponding variables in the NASDAQ regressions. Four of the coefficients of Assets are positive and significant at the 5 percent level or better. Also, the coefficients of PPE are all positive and four are significant at the 5 percent level or better. The coefficients of Tobin's q are all negative and significant at the 1 percent level. For Std. ROA, the coefficients are all negative and four are significant at the 1 percent level. This result is somewhat stronger for the NYSE firms than for NASDAQ firms. In general, these regressions indicate that there are strong relationships between firm size (direct), collateral availability (direct), growth opportunities (inverse), and firm risk (inverse) and the amount of debt in a firm's capital structure for both NYSE and NASDAQ firms. The main difference between the two sets of regressions relates to firm profitability. While there was little or no relationship between profitability and capital structure for NASDAQ firms, there is a strong inverse relationship for NYSE firms. For NYSE firms, four of the coefficients of ROA are negative and significant at the 1 percent level. For Avg. ROA, the coefficients are all negative and three are significant at the 1 percent level. These results indicate that the amount of debt in NYSE firms' capital structures is inversely related to both current and long-term profitability. This result is consistent with Myers and Majluf's "asymmetric information theory" of capital structure.

To this point, two of the main results of this study are that NYSE firms have more debt in their capital structures than NASDAQ firms and that profitability and capital structure are inversely related for NYSE firms but not for NASDAQ firms. These findings will be further tested in a regres-

Table 9.3
Regression Analysis of Capital Structure for NASDAQ Firms

	1985	1989	1994	1999	2003
Intercept	.157c	.196c	.154c	.104c	.082c
(t value)	(7.53)	(9.73)	(13.1)	(13.3)	(13.8)
Assets (10^4)	.147c	.074c	.046c	.046c	.032c
	(3.31)	(2.93)	(4.37)	(3.82)	(3.47)
PPE	.188c	.220c	.234c	.295c	.298c
	(4.07)	(5.19)	(9.25)	(13.8)	(16.4)
Tobin's q	-.008b	-.020c	-.021c	-.003c	-.002c
	(-2.35)	(-4.63)	(-7.79)	(-6.47)	(-3.43)
ROA	-.054	-.020	.190c	-.042	.016
	(-.054)	(-0.20)	(3.13)	(-1.06)	(0.53)
Avg. ROA	-.144	-.242a	-.301c	-.015	-.060a
	(-1.07)	(-1.71)	(-4.13)	(-0.35)	(-1.89)
Std. ROA	-.160a	-.133	-.193c	-.006	-.054b
	(-1.72)	(-1.39)	(-3.83)	(-0.19)	(-2.14)
Adj. R^2	.11	.13	.23	.18	.16
F value	7.33c	10.9c	36.3c	49.2c	52.2c

a = significant at the 10% level
b = significant at the 5% level
c = significant at the 1% level

sion analysis in which both NYSE and NASDAQ firms are included in each sample year's regression. This will allow us to test for the statistical significance of the above findings. This will require that two new independent variables be employed. The first is NasdD, a dummy variable that takes on a value of one if the sample firm is a NASDAQ firm and zero otherwise. The coefficient of this dummy variable will indicate whether there is a difference in the amount of debt in the capital structures of the two groups of firms. The second new variable is ROA·NasdD (ROA multiplied by NasdD), an interactive dummy variable that will indicate whether there is a difference in the relationship between profitability and firm capital structure for the two groups of sample firms. The results of these regressions are presented in table 9.5. The coefficients of Assets, PPE, Tobin's q, Std. ROA, ROA, and Avg. ROA are similar to those reported previously. The coefficient of NasdD is negative and significant at the 1% level in all regressions. This indicates that, on average, NASDAQ firms use less debt in their capital structures than NYSE firms. The coefficients show that after controlling for firm size, profitability, etc. NASDAQ firms have averaged 8 percent to 10 percent less debt in their capital structures than NYSE firms over the last decade. The coefficients of ROA·NasdD are all positive and significant at the 1 percent level. This indicates that there is a statistically significant difference in the relationship between profitability and capital structure for the two groups of sample firms. The coefficient of ROA shows this relationship for NYSE firms and indicates a statistically significant inverse relationship between profitability and capital structure in all sample years. The sum of the coefficients of ROA and ROA·NasdD shows the relationship for NASDAQ firms. For example, for 2003 the sum of the coefficients is .051 (-.377 + .428). Since .051 is not statistically significant at conventional levels ($t = 0.63$), this means that there is no relationship between profitability and capital structure for NASDAQ firms. The same is true for all other sample years. In sum, these regressions indicate there is a strong inverse relationship between profitability and the amount of debt in a firm's capital structure for NYSE firms and no relationship between the two variables for NASDAQ firms.

Concluding Remarks

Our study shows that the firms belonging to the NYSE on average have higher debt ratios than firms belonging to the NASDAQ market. But the debt ratios for the Nasdaq firms went down significantly, while for firms in the NYSE they remained relatively stable during 1985-2003. Also, while

Table 9.4
Regression Analysis of Capital Structure for NYSE Firms

	1985	1989	1994	1999	2003
Intercept	.262c	.339c	.298c	.321c	.298c
(t value)	(14.5)	(18.5)	(19.4)	(25.8)	(25.2)
Assets (10^4)	-.010	.013c	.008b	.005b	.004c
	(-1.18)	(3.00)	(2.55)	(2.18)	(3.33)
PPE	.127c	.049	.059b	.092c	.107c
	(3.77)	(1.58)	(2.41)	(4.26)	(5.59)
Tobin's q	-.017c	-.020c	-.018c	-.010c	-.020c
	(-2.86)	(-2.71)	(-3.11)	(-5.17)	(-4.98)
ROA	-.472c	-.862c	-.628c	-.317c	.006
	(-3.28)	(-5.33)	(-4.57)	(-2.82)	(0.06)
Avg. ROA	-.272	-.029	-.354c	-.647c	-.728c
	(-1.35)	(-0.16)	(-2.73)	(-5.47)	(-5.64)
Std. ROA	-.683c	-.768c	-.071	-.356c	-.793c
	(-3.45)	(-4.06)	(-0.53)	(-3.14)	(-6.07)
Adj. R^2	.21	.24	.24	.21	.19
F value	21.7c	28.5c	34.7c	38.6c	37.9c

a = significant at the 10% level
b = significant at the 5% level
c = significant at the 1% level

Table 9.5
Regression Analysis of Capital Structure for NYSE and NASDAQ Firms

	1985	1989	1994	1999	2003
Intercept	.227c	.291c	.266c	.240c	.184c
(t value)	(14.9)	(18.6)	(22.6)	(24.2)	(23.5)
Assets (10^4)	.001	.017c	.012c	.007c	.006c
	(0.10)	(3.70)	(3.81)	(3.15)	(4.20)
PPE	.137c	.122c	.151c	.212c	.226c
	(5.07)	(4.72)	(8.49)	(13.5)	(16.6)
Tobin's q	-.011c	-.020c	-.021c	-.004c	-.002c
	(-4.02)	(-5.69)	(-8.92)	(-8.58)	(-4.57)
NasdD	-.038c	-.060c	-.088c	-.106c	-.080c
	(-2.99)	(-4.42)	(-8.38)	(-11.8)	(-10.9)
ROA	-.489c	-.651c	-.575c	-.675c	-.377c
	(-4.33)	(-4.63)	(-5.37)	(-7.32)	(-4.80)
ROA·NasdD	.465c	.588c	.757c	.685c	.428c
	(3.92)	(4.27)	(7.18)	(7.29)	(3.74)
Avg. ROA	-.211b	-.229b	-.294c	-.088b	-.112c
	(-2.02)	(-2.17)	(-4.88)	(-2.22)	(-3.74)
Std. ROA	-.223c	-.172b	-.189c	-.059b	-.098c
	(-3.00)	(-2.31)	(-4.47)	(-2.06)	(-4.09)
Adj. R^2	.15	.17	.25	.22	.19
F value	17.0c	23.6c	57.6c	79.7c	78.8c

a = significant at the 10% level
b = significant at the 5% level
c = significant at the 1% level

there is a strong inverse relationship between profitability and the amount of debt in the capital structure of NYSE firms, no such relationship was found between these two variables for the NASDAQ firms.

References

Berger, P., E. Ofek, and D. Yermack, (1997), "Managerial Entrenchment and Capital Structure Decisions," *Journal of Finance*, Vol. 52, No. 4, pp. 1411-38.

Fama, E. and K. French, (2001), "Disappearing Dividends: Changing Firm Character Tics or Lower Propensity to Pay," *Journal of Financial Economics*, Vol. 60, 3-43.

Friend, I. and L. Lang, (1988), "An Empirical Test of the Impact of Managerial Self-Interest on Corporate Capital Structure," *Journal of Finance*, Vol. 43, No. 2, pp. 271-81.

Jensen, M. (1986) "Agency Costs of Free Cash Flow, Corporate Finance, and Takeovers." *American Economic Review*, Vol. 76, 323-329.

Myers, S. (1984), "The Capital Structure Puzzle," *Journal of Finance*, Vol. 39, No. 3, 575-92.

Myers, S. and N. Majluf, (1984), "Corporate Financing and Investment Decisions When Firms Have Information That Investors Do Not Have," *Journal of Financial Economics*, Vol. 13, 187-221.

10

Capital Structure and Firm Profitability: NYSE and AMEX Firms

In a recent study, Fama and French (2001) showed that over the last twenty or so years a large number of companies have stopped paying dividends to their common stockholders'. Specifically, in 1978, 66.5 percent of publicly-traded firms paid dividends but by 1999 only 20.8 percent of such firms paid dividends. In analyzing their data, Fama and French conclude that part of the reason for the declining dividend payments has been a general reduction in the propensity of firms to pay dividends. One possible explanation for this reduction in the propensity to pay is that firms have decided to rely more on internally-generated funds to finance their investment opportunities than they have in the past. Formally, this is the "pecking order theory" of firm capital structure suggested by Myers (1984) and Myers and Majluf (1984). Assuming the "pecking order theory" is the correct explanation of the dividend reductions firms will, among other things, also be using less debt capital to finance their investments than they have in the past. Fosberg and Ghosh (2005) tested this theory on a large sample of NYSE and NASDAQ firms and found that there had been a significant reduction in the amount of debt in the capital structures of NASDAQ firms over the last twenty years. NYSE firms did not exhibit any noticeable changes in capital structure over the period. At this point it is unclear if this difference in capital structure changes is due to firm size, exchange listing, or some other factor. Additionally, Fosberg and Ghosh found that there is a significant inverse relationship between firm profitability and the amount of debt in the firm's capital structure for NYSE firms, but not for NASDAQ firms.

In this study, we seek to extend previous research by ascertaining if the capital structure and profitability effects noted above extend to firms listed on the AMEX as well. We will also seek to determine what factors are causing these profitability and capital structure effects.

Data and Sample Selection

Our base sample is all firms listed on the NYSE and AMEX stock markets that are reported on the *COMPUSTAT* database (10-29-04 version). Firms in the utilities and financial services industries were eliminated from the base sample because of the potential biases associated with the heavy regulation of those industries. Companies with negative net worths in any sample year were also eliminated from the base sample because of the distorted capital structures of these firms. Outliers, firms with return on assets of more than 100 percent or less than -100 percent in any sample year, were also eliminated from the base sample. This resulted in a final sample of 1,022 NYSE and 244 AMEX firms. Data for each sample company for the sample years 1985, 1989, 1994, 1999, and 2003 was obtained from *COMPUSTAT*. Some companies did not have data for every sample year. Data for NASDAQ firms cited in this study came from Fosberg and Ghosh (2005). Previous studies such as Friend and Lang (1988) and Berger, Ofek, and Yermack (1997) have shown that the amount of debt in a firm's capital structure is affected by a number of factors including primarily firm size, risk, collateral availability, and growth opportunities. We will control for all of these factors in our analysis. Our firm size proxies are total assets (Assets), sales (Sales), and the market value of common equity (MVE). Collateral availability is measure by the firm's net property, plant, and equipment to total assets ratio (PPE). Growth opportunities are measured by the market to book value of common equity (MVE/BE) and Tobin's q. Tobin's q is calculated as the sum of the book values of debt and preferred equity plus the market value of common equity divided by the sum of the book values of debt, preferred, and common equity.

There are two well-known theories that seek to explain the relationship between profitability and the amount of debt in a firm's capital structure. Jensen (1986) believes that greater profitability should result in more debt usage by firms in order to control the agency costs associated with free cash flow. Specifically, the increased debt service requirements caused by additional debt will force managers to pay out more of the firm's free cash flows to creditors and leave less money for managers to use for things that do not benefit the firm's shareholders. Jensen's theory implies a direct relationship between profitability and the amount of debt in a firm's capital structure. Myers and Majluf (1984), however, argue that if there is asymmetric information in the capital markets, new security issues (debt and equity) will be undervalued by investors and the firm will be better off financing its investments with internally-generated funds. Firms will, therefore, only finance with outside debt capital when internally-generated funds are insufficient to fully fund the firm's investment opportunities. Myers and Majluf's theory implies an inverse relationship between profitability and the amount of debt in the firm's capital structure. Our empirical analysis should indicate which of these two theories is correct. Additionally, we will test to see if the relationship between firm profitability and the amount of debt in the typical firm's capital structure has changed over the last twenty years. Profitability is measured by sample year return on assets (ROA), return on equity (ROE), and operating cash flow divided by total assets (CF/Assets). Firm risk is measured by the standard deviation of ROA, ROE, and CF/Assets over the five-year period from sample year t to year t – 4.

Empirical Results

The mean values of selected variables for the AMEX sample firms for each of the sample years are presented in table 10.1. Looking first at the size proxies, it is evident that the average size of AMEX firms grew only slightly over the sample period. For example, mean Assets grew from $254 million in 1985 to only $318 million in 2003. Also, there is a decrease in the amount of debt in the AMEX firms' capital structures over the sample period. The mean total debt to total assets ratio (Debt/Assets) declined from .208 in 1985 to .174 in 2003. Similarly, the mean total debt to total capital ratio (Debt/T. Cap.) dropped from .269 in 1985 to .232 in 2003. Total capital is the sum of the book values of debt, preferred, and common equity. Interestingly, firm profitability has also decreased over the sample period. Mean ROA for the sample firms dropped from .049 (4.9 percent) in 1985 to -.045 in 2003. Similar decreases in ROE and CF/Assets are also evident. The data shows that AMEX firms' growth opportunities have increased over time as both mean MVE/BE and Tobin's q have risen over the sample period. Mean PPE increased from .274 in 1985 to .290 in 2003, indicating that AMEX firms have slightly more collateral available to pledge on debt than they used to.

NYSE firms display many, but not all, of the trends exhibited by AMEX firms (see table 10.2). For example, mean Assets grew substantially over the sample period from $2.463 billion in 1985 to $8.678 billion in 2003. Also, comparing mean Assets figures, it is evident that the average NYSE firm is more than ten times larger than the average AMEX firm. The mean profitability of the NYSE firms has also declined over the sample period. For example, mean ROA declined from .060 (6.0

percent) in 1985 to .042 in 2003. Other profitability measures exhibit a similar trend. Growth opportunities for NYSE firms have also increased as indicated by the increase in MVE/BE from 2.18 in 1985 to 2.69 in 2003. There has also been a slight decline in collateral availability (PPE) in recent years. The one trend that is different for NYSE firms relates to their capital structures. Examining the Debt/Assets ratio, the decrease in the amount of debt in AMEX firms' capital structures is not evident for NYSE firms. In fact, there is no discernible trend in the capital structures of NYSE firms. However, the typical NYSE firm has, on average, more debt in its capital structure in each sample year than the average AMEX firm (5 percent more over the last decade).

Our next objective is to test for the relationship, if any, between firm profitability and capital structure and to see if this relationship has changed over time. This will be accomplished with a regression analysis in which the firm's Debt/Assets ratio is used as the dependent variable. A separate regression will be run for each sample year. In each regres-

Table 10.1
Summary Statistics for Selected Variables for the AMEX Firms

Panel A: Firm Size					
	1985	1989	1994	1999	2003
Assets ($M)	254	364	607	320	318
Sales ($M)	269	313	296	328	361
MVE ($M)	196	358	200	199	355
Panel B: Capital Structure					
Debt ($M)	53	97	78	104	103
Debt/Assets	.208	.237	.194	.228	.174
Debt/T. Cap.	.269	.301	.256	.299	.232
Panel C: Profitability, Growth, etc.					
ROA	.049	.021	.013	-.009	-.045
ROE	.076	.036	.032	.002	-.067
CF/Assets	.126	.098	.088	.051	.012
MVE/BE	2.41	1.86	2.00	3.01	3.26
Tobin's q	1.09	1.61	1.77	2.71	3.00
PPE	.274	.300	.313	.315	.290

M = million

sion, control variables for firm size, collateral, growth opportunities, and risk will be employed. The main independent variables of interest are profitability measures (ROA and Avg. ROA). ROA measures current year profitability while Avg. ROA (average annual ROA over years t to t - 4) measures long-term profitability. In table 10.3, the results of the regressions for AMEX firms are presented. In these regressions, firm size (Assets) is weakly correlated with the amount of debt in the sample firms' capital structures. In four of the sample year regressions, the coefficient of Assets is positive but not significant at conventional levels. Collateral availability is shown to be a significant determinant of firm capital structure. The coefficients of PPE are all positive and two are significant at the 10 percent level or better. Four of the coefficients of Tobin's q are negative and three of these are significant at the 10 percent level or better. This indicates that high-growth firms tend to use less debt in their capital structures than low-growth firms. Firm risk does not seem to be an important determinant of firm capital structure as the coefficients of Std. ROA do not have a consistent sign. The relationship between firm profitability and capital structure is also weak, at best. Looking at current year's profitability (ROA), only one coefficient is statistically significant at conventional levels and the signs of the coefficients are not consistent. For long-term profitability (Avg. ROA), the coefficients are again inconsistent in their signs. In sum, these results indicate there is little or no relationship between firm profitability and the amount of debt in AMEX firms' capital structures.

Other dependent and control variables were also tried in the above regressions (not shown). Sales and MVE were tried as size proxies and ROE and CF/Assets were used as profitability measures. Additionally, MVE/BE was employed as a growth proxy and Debt/T. Cap. was substituted as the capital structure proxy. None of these variables improved on the explanatory power of the regressions reported above.

Table 10.4 contains the results of a similar regression analysis performed on NYSE firms. Four of the coefficients of Assets are positive and significant at the 5% level or better. Also, the coefficients of PPE are all positive and four are significant at the 5 percent level or better. The coefficients of Tobin's q are all negative and significant at the 1 percent level. For Std. ROA, the coefficients are all negative and four are significant at the 1 percent level. These results are much stronger for the NYSE firms than they were for the AMEX firms. In general, these regressions indicate that there are strong relationships between firm size (direct), collateral availability (direct), growth opportunities (inverse),

Table 10.2
Summary Statistics for Selected Variables for the NYSE Firms

	1985	1989	1994	1999	2003
Panel A: Firm Size					
Assets ($M)	2463	4075	4767	6247	8678
Sales ($M)	2830	3759	4297	5450	7163
MVE ($M)	1868	2808	3508	9074	8416
Panel B: Capital Structure					
Debt ($M)	536	1355	1399	1929	2571
Debt/Assets	.215	.251	.230	.269	.239
Debt/T. Cap.	.296	.346	.327	.373	.344
Panel C: Profitability, Growth, etc.					
ROA	.060	.062	.062	.054	.042
ROE	.115	.128	.131	.127	.092
CF/Assets	.164	.160	.161	.153	.133
MVE/BE	2.18	2.30	2.55	3.16	2.69
Tobin's q	1.88	1.89	2.08	2.42	2.08
PPE	.368	.368	.374	.356	.338

M = million

and firm risk (inverse) and the amount of debt in a firm's capital structure for NYSE firms. Another significant difference between the two sets of regressions relates to firm profitability. While there was little or no relationship between profitability and capital structure for AMEX firms, there is a strong inverse relationship for NYSE firms. For NYSE firms, four of the coefficients of ROA are negative and significant at the 1 percent level. For Avg. ROA, the coefficients are all negative and three are significant at the 1 percent level. These results indicate that the amount of debt in NYSE firms' capital structures is inversely related to both current and long-term profitability. This result is consistent with Myers and Majluf's "asymmetric information theory" of capital structure.

To this point, two of the main results of this study are that NYSE firms have more debt in their capital structures than AMEX firms and that profitability and capital structure are inversely related for NYSE firms but not for AMEX firms. These findings will be further tested in a regression analysis in which both NYSE and AMEX firms are included

Table 10.3
Regression Analysis of Capital Structure for AMEX Firms

	1985	1989	1994	1999	2003
Intercept	.237c	.344c	.216c	.248c	.170c
(t value)	(4.68)	(6.88)	(5.53)	(7.25)	(8.19)
Assets (10^4)	.014	.015	-.013	.071	.080
	(0.13)	(0.18)	(-0.48)	(1.03)	(1.64)
PPE	.051	.018	.136a	.025	.149c
	(0.49)	(0.18)	(1.72)	(0.41)	(3.16)
Tobin's q	-.001	.001	-.019a	-.018c	-.014c
	(-0.06)	(0.03)	(-1.83)	(-3.14)	(-4.28)
ROA	-1.76c	-.435	.215	.278	-.048
	(-5.30)	(-1.32)	(1.15)	(-1.06)	(-0.49)
Avg. ROA	.889b	-.900b	-.503a	-.344	.052
	(2.19)	(-2.10)	(-1.77)	(-1.39)	(0.53)
Std. ROA	.246	-1.62c	-.498b	.096	.032
	(0.45)	(-3.24)	(-2.01)	(0.44)	(0.46)
Adj. R^2	.23	.12	.08	.04	.13
F value	5.30c	3.20c	2.65b	2.14a	6.29c

a = significant at the 10% level
b = significant at the 5% level
c = significant at the 1% level

in each sample year's regression. This will allow us to test for the statistical significance of the above findings. This will require that two new independent variables be employed. The first is NasdD, a dummy variable that takes on a value of one if the sample firm is an AMEX firm and zero otherwise. The coefficient of this dummy variable will indicate whether there is a difference in the amount of debt in the capital structures of the two groups of firms. The second new variable is ROA·NasdD (ROA multiplied by NasdD), an interactive dummy variable that will indicate whether there is a difference in the relationship between profitability and firm capital structure for the two groups of sample firms.

The results of these regressions are presented in table 10.5. The coefficients of Assets, PPE, Tobin's q, Std. ROA, ROA, and Avg. ROA are similar to those reported previously in table 10.4. The coefficient of NasdD is negative in four years and three of those are significant at the 1 percent level. This indicates that, on average, AMEX firms use less debt in their capital structures than NYSE firms. The coefficients show that after controlling for firm size, profitability, etc. AMEX firms have averaged 5 percent to 8 percent less debt in their capital structures than NYSE firms over the last decade. Four of the coefficients of ROA·NasdD are positive and three of those are significant at the 1 percent level. This indicates that there is a statistically-significant difference in the relationship between profitability and capital structure for the two groups of sample firms. The coefficient of ROA shows this relationship for NYSE firms and indicates a statistically-significant inverse relationship between profitability and capital structure in all sample years. The sum of the coefficients of ROA and ROA·NasdD shows the relationship between profitability and capital structure for AMEX firms. For example, for 2003 the sum of the coefficients is .137 (-.178 + .315). Since .137 is not statistically significant at conventional levels (t = 0.95), this means that there is no relationship between profitability and capital structure for AMEX firms in 2003. Overall, the sum of the coefficients is positive in the last three sample years (one is significant) and negative in the first two sample years (both are significant). In sum, the erratic signs of the coefficient sums indicate there is no consistent relationship between profitability and capital structure for AMEX firms.

Fosberg and Ghosh (2005) did an analysis of NASDAQ firms for the same sample years used in this study and found results similar to those that we report for AMEX firms. For example, NASDAQ firms have mean Assets over the sample years of $574 million versus $373 million for AMEX firms. Thus, AMEX and NASDAQ firms are of approximately the same size whereas NYSE firms are much larger (mean Assets of $5.246 billion). NASDAQ firms also experience a similar decline in the amount of debt in their capital structures (from Debt/Assets of .204 in 1985 to .141 in 2003) as noted above for AMEX firms. Also, NASDAQ firms are found to exhibit no relationship between firm profitability and the amount of debt in their capital structures. The similarity of these results suggests several implications. First, the lack of a relationship between profitability and capital structure is not an exchange listing phenomenon as it is apparent for both NASDAQ and AMEX firms. Similarly, the lower debt usage by both NASDAQ and AMEX firms can not be an exchange listing phenomenon. The results of this study do not suggest what the cause of these anomalies might be and, therefore, that is left to future research.

Table 10.4
Regression Analysis of Capital Structure for NYSE Firms

	1985	1989	1994	1999	2003
Intercept	.262c	.339c	.298c	.321c	.298c
(t value)	(14.5)	(18.5)	(19.4)	(25.8)	(25.2)
Assets (10^4)	-.010	.013c	.008b	.005b	.004c
	(-1.18)	(3.00)	(2.55)	(2.18)	(3.33)
PPE	.127c	.049	.059b	.092c	.107c
	(3.77)	(1.58)	(2.41)	(4.26)	(5.59)
Tobin's q	-.017c	-.020c	-.018c	-.010c	-.020c
	(-2.86)	(-2.71)	(-3.11)	(-5.17)	(-4.98)
ROA	-.472c	-.862c	-.628c	-.317c	.006
	(-3.28)	(-5.33)	(-4.57)	(-2.82)	(0.06)
Avg. ROA	-.272	-.029	-.354c	-.647c	-.728c
	(-1.35)	(-0.16)	(-2.73)	(-5.47)	(-5.64)
Std. ROA	-.683c	-.768c	-.071	-.356c	-.793c
	(-3.45)	(-4.06)	(-0.53)	(-3.14)	(-6.07)
Adj. R^2	.21	.24	.24	.21	.19
F value	21.7c	28.5c	34.7c	38.6c	37.9c

a = t-values significant at the 10% level
b = t-values significant at the 5% level
c = t-values significant at the 1% level

Concluding Remarks

In this chapter, we have reached almost the same conclusions as in chapter 9—that firms traded on the NYSE generally use more debt in their capital structures than firms listed on the AMEX. Also, the debt ratios of the sample firms listed on the NYSE declined somewhat during 1985-2003 while firms traded on the AMEX market had relatively stable debt ratios. Moreover, for the NYSE firms, there is a strong negative relationship between a firm's debt ratio and profitability, whereas no such relationship is found for the AMEX firms. Comparison of these results to similar calculations found in Fosberg and Ghosh (2005) for NASDAQ

Table 10.5
Regression Analysis of Capital Structure for AMEX and NYSE Firms

	1985	1989	1994	1999	2003
Intercept	.251c	.340c	.300c	.320c	.255c
(t value)	(14.2)	(19.0)	(22.6)	(25.7)	(25.5)
Assets (10^4)	-.008	.013c	.007b	.005b	.005c
	(-0.91)	(2.85)	(2.23)	(2.27)	(3.53)
PPE	.110c	.042	.072c	.077c	.119c
	(3.54)	(1.38)	(3.04)	(3.73)	(6.54)
Tobin's q	-.013c	-.011a	-.019c	-.012c	-.019c
	(-2.64)	(-1.79)	(-3.84)	(-6.50)	(-8.36)
NasdD	.031	-.029	-.084c	-.077c	-.048c
	(1.61)	(-1.55)	(-5.30)	(-5.42)	(-4.04)
ROA	-.658c	-.786c	-.680c	-.355c	-.178b
	(-4.85)	(-4.83)	(-5.36)	(-3.22)	(-2.14)
ROA·NasdD	-.595b	.174	.785c	.743c	.315c
	(3.92)	(0.80)	(5.26)	(5.71)	(3.15)
Avg. ROA	-.032	-.315b	-.283c	-.517c	-.229c
	(-2.02)	(-1.97)	(-2.84)	(-5.21)	(-3.28)
Std. ROA	-.556c	-.922c	-.269c	-.206b	-.167c
	(-3.01)	(-5.17)	(-2.84)	(-2.13)	(-3.37)
Adj. R^2	.21	.21	.21	.17	.16
F value	18.7c	21.7c	26.9c	27.3c	29.0c

a = significant at the 10% level
b = significant at the 5% level
c = significant at the 1% level

firms shows that, like AMEX firms, NASDAQ firms use less debt in their capital structures than NYSE firms and exhibit no relationship between profitability and capital structure. Consequently, because these anomalies exist for both AMEX and NASDAQ firms, these two anomalies can not be an exchange listing effect.

References

Berger, P., E. Ofek, and D. Yermack, (1997), "Managerial Entrenchment and Capital Structure Decisions," *Journal of Finance*, Vol. 52, No. 4, pp. 1411-38.

Fama, E. and K. French, (2001), "Disappearing Dividends: Changing Firm Characteristics or Lower Propensity to Pay," *Journal of Financial Economics*, Vol. 60, 3-43.

Fosberg, R. and A. Ghosh, (2005), "Capital Structure Changes in NYSE and NASDAQ Firms," Working Paper, William Paterson University.

Friend, I. and L. Lang, (1988), "An Empirical Test of the Impact of Managerial Self-Interest on Corporate Capital Structure," *Journal of Finance*, Vol. 43, No. 2, pp. 271-81.

Jensen, M. (1986), "Agency Costs of Free Cash Flow, Corporate Finance, and Takeovers." *American Economic Review*, Vol. 76, 323-329.

Myers, S. (1984), "The Capital Structure Puzzle," *Journal of Finance*, Vol. 39, No. 3, 575-92.

Myers, S. and N. Majluf, (1984), "Corporate Financing and Investment Decisions When Firms Have Information That Investors Do Not Have," *Journal of Financial Economics*, Vol. 13, 187-221.

11

Summary and Conclusions

Summary of the Study

In chapter 1, we have given an overview of the capital structure controversy. We have shown that the assumptions of the Modigliani-Miller hypothesis are too simplistic to apply to the real world. When the noted assumption is relaxed, then we find the impossible situation that the firms should borrow up to the hilt (i.e., 100 percent) to minimize their tax burdens. This being an impossibility in the face of bankruptcy costs and other risks, there evolves the optimal capital structure theory where the risk-return combination works in such a way that the value of the firm is maximized and the weighted average cost of capital is minimized. But the competing Pecking Order Theory contends that firms go for the internal financing capital first, and when the need for external capital arises, they opt for the debt capital first and finance with equity capital as the last resort. While some aspects of each theory are true, they are far from perfect and their empirical verification is still lacking. They are conditional theories of capital structure and are not designed to be generally accurate. Thus the testing of these two competing theories becomes the prime task of any treatise on capital structure.

In chapter 2, the empirical results show that firms will adjust their capital structure toward the industry mean when it is above the mean. But the probability that firms will adjust their capital structure toward the industry mean is very low when it is below the mean, indicating that firms are indifferent to the debt level as long as it is below the industry mean. To explain this phenomenon, we developed the concept of optimal capital structure range within which a typical U.S. firm will be indifferent to its debt level. The empirical results strongly suggest that the likelihood a firm will use the internal financing as opposed to the external financing is very high. Furthermore, when a firm needs external financing, it generally prefers debt to equity. Our study thus shows that both the optimal capital structure hypothesis and the pecking order hypothesis coexist and that they are not mutually exclusive, as Claggett, Jr. had found. But the pecking order hypothesis is more pronounced than the optimal capital structure hypothesis as the former was significant for all the industries and for all the years, while the latter was significant for the majority of industries and for the majority of the years covered by our study.

Why does a firm adjust the capital structure toward the industry mean when it is above the mean, while it is indifferent when the capital structure is below the mean? One possible explanation for this is as follows: when a firm's debt level reaches a significantly high level, the high cost of the debt associated with the high leverage makes the reduction of the debt a meaningful task. But the firms that have below average debt levels do not put the consideration of debt level as their first priority. Some other factors, such as the availability of the funds and market conditions may also play an important role in the consideration of the firm's capital structure.

In chapter 3, we study whether a firm's capital structure follows the optimal capital structure theory or pecking order theory. Using the industry mean as a predicator of a firm's capital structure, we have constructed three hypotheses and have used a binomial model to perform the empirical tests on the financial data of *Fortune 500* manufacturing companies. The first finding in this chapter shows that, in general, the probability that a firm's debt level is moving toward the industry's mean is not significantly different from the probability that it is moving further away from the industry mean. Also, the probability that a firm's debt level is moving toward the industry's mean is very high when it is above the industry mean. Moreover, our study suggests that the optimal capital structure is not a single point; rather, it is a range of values from zero to the industry mean within which a typical U.S. firm will be indifferent to the firm's debt level. In other words, a firm will only adjust to the optimal capital structure when the firm's debt level is out of this range. The second result of our analysis generally agrees with the pecking order theory, that is, firms prefer using internal financing as opposed to using external financing. The third finding is that, when external funds are required, a firm prefers debt financing to equity financing.

Chapter 4 partly answers the question of "What determines corporate leverage?" posed in the introduction. We use nine independent variables, business risk, and industry dummies in our analysis. First, our results confirm the usefulness of taking growth of assets, fixed asset ratio, R

& D expenditure and advertising expenditure as the determinants of capital structure. Secondly, our results show the rather insignificant role of industry dummies as a proxy for industry characteristics in capital structure determination. And finally, the results show that the relationship between business risk and leverage is quadratic, and it is first increasing and then decreasing.

We would like to point out that in our results some of the independent variables show the expected sign and statistical significance, while some other variables either have not shown the expected sign or have the expected sign but no statistical significance. Furthermore, for some variables, the signs and importance vary at different time periods. The problem of omitted variables remains as the known determinants "explain" only a small percentage of the variation in capital structure. All this indicates that nothing is "settled" in the area of the determinants of capital structure, and much work is to be done if we want to understand what truly determines the capital structure of a firm or an industry.

In chapter 5, our results have shown that there is no systematic relationship between industrial concentration and debt ratios of firms belonging to that industry, as had been found by Melicher, Rush, and Winn in their study. We have also found no evidence that firms differing in market power have different debt ratios, contrary to the findings by Lyn and Papaioannou. Obviously, firms with high industry concentration do not respond to factors that affect debt policy differently when they set their debt ratios.

When we analyze the regression results, we find that only four out of six regression equations have negative signs when the debt ratio was the dependent variable, but only three were statistically significant. Also, they were not in ascending order, as the underlying theory stipulates. The same was true when the slack variable (cash and equivalents) was used as the dependent variable. They were also not in ascending order in their values with the respective concentration class. Thus we have found no consistent relationship between industrial concentration and debt ratios of firms belonging to that industry, respectively. Firms with a higher degree of concentration do not exercise more restraint in their debt ratios than more competitive firms. Our results thus contradict the findings obtained by Lyn and Papaioannou, and leaves room for further research in this vital area of capital structure.

The main conclusion of chapter 6 is that the stock prices of most companies go down significantly when a firm announces a substantial amount of new stock offerings that merit separate mentioning in the *Wall Street*

Journal or similar financial publications. For the firms covered by this study, the average abnormal return of firms on the day of announcement was –7.35 percent, while the cumulative average abnormal return for the entire observation period was –11.47 percent. Thus the announcement of major stock offering by the firms generally has a chilling effect on stock prices, as the adverse signaling effect and the impact of potential dilution of stock ownership as well as the situation of oversupply as compared to the demand become more pronounced to the investing public.

When we divide our sample firms into the firms belonging to the New York Stock Exchange (NYSE), and those belonging to the over-the-counter (OTC.) market, we find that the average abnormal return on the announcement date was negative for the NYSE firms, but positive for the OTC firms. The cumulative average abnormal return for the entire observation period was also negative for the firms belonging to the NYSE, but was positive for the OTC firms. It seems that the adverse impact of new stock offerings was limited to the more established firms as compared to those relatively new and smaller capitalized firms.

Similarly, when we divide our entire time period into two sub-periods, namely mildly bullish (1990-1993), and strongly bullish (1994-1997), we find that the average abnormal return for firms during 1990-1993 was negative on the announcement date, but positive during 1994-1997. The cumulative average abnormal return for the entire observation period also showed the same pattern, that is, negative for the first sub-period but positive for the second sub-period. Thus the extremely robust stock market in conjunction with the very strong economy was able to negate the adverse impact of new stock offerings during the more recent period of our unprecedented bull market.

In chapter 7, we have found that there was a positive and statistically-significant association between the salary and bonus of the CEOs of the 336 largest U.S. corporations, and the debts these firms incurred during the 1989-1999 time period. This was also true when total compensation (which included realized stock options) of the CEOs was taken as the dependent variable, although the latter was less effective than the former one. Also, both three-year average sales growth and one-year stock price return showed promises as the explanatory variables in most of the equations, but unfortunately, net income and size did not perform at all as the explanatory variables in these equations during the period covered by our study.

It is interesting to note that the b-values of the capital structure variable were higher in 1999 than they were in 1989 for all the equations when both salary and bonus, and total compensation were used as the dependent variables. But the dummy variables used as proxies for industry characteristics (i.e., manufacturing vs. service industries) were not significant at all in any of the regression equations.

Our study thus shows that if higher leverage of a firm is viewed as growth opportunities to be reflected in higher profits and higher stock returns of these companies, then higher executive salary (including bonus) is taken as a reward for higher risk taking and further growth of firms. The risk-return relationship also prevails in this area of capital structure and executive compensation.

In chapter 8, we have attempted to determine whether a firm's ownership structure affects its capital structure and whether these effects are the same for NYSE and NASDAQ firms. Our results indicate that there is an inverse relationship between managerial share ownership and the percentage of debt in the firm's capital structure for NYSE firms. No relationship was found between managerial share ownership and firm capital structure for NASDAQ firms. Additionally, a direct relationship was found between blockholder share ownership and the amount of debt financing a firm employs for both NYSE and NASDAQ firms. These results are largely consistent with extant ownership and capital structure theories. It was also found that NASDAQ firms, on average, employ less debt in their capital structures and have higher managerial and blockholder share ownership than NYSE firms. We also found that between 1993 and 2000, NYSE firms experienced a decrease in the amount of debt in their capital structures and an increase in blockholder share ownership.

In chapter 9, we found that NYSE and NASDAQ firms have somewhat different capital structures. NYSE firms generally use 8 percent to 10 percent more debt financing in their capital structures than NASDAQ firms. It was also found that the amount of debt in the capital structures of NASDAQ firms declined significantly between 1985 and 2003 but remained relatively stable for NYSE firms. Also, NYSE firms were found to exhibit a strong inverse relationship between firm profitability and the amount of debt in the firm's capital structure. This result is generally consistent with the Myers and Majluf's "asymmetric information theory" of capital structure. No relationship was found between profitability and capital structure for NASDAQ firms.

In chapter 10, we found that NYSE and AMEX firms have somewhat different capital structures. NYSE firms generally use 5 percent to 8 percent more debt financing in their capital structures than AMEX firms. It was also found that the amount of debt in the capital structures of AMEX firms declined somewhat between 1985 and 2003 but remained relatively stable for NYSE firms. Also, NYSE firms were found to exhibit a strong inverse relationship between firm profitability and the amount of debt in the firm's capital structure. This result is generally consistent with Myers and Majluf's "asymmetric information theory" of capital structure. No relationship was found between profitability and capital structure for AMEX firms. Comparison of these results to similar calculations found in Fosberg and Ghosh (2005) for NASDAQ firms shows that, like AMEX firms, NASDAQ firms use less debt in their capital structures than NYSE firms and exhibit no relationship between profitability and capital structure. Consequently, because these anomalies exist for both AMEX and NASDAQ firms, these two anomalies can not be an exchange listing effect.

In a nutshell, evidence in support of both the optimal capital structure theory and the pecking order theory exist, but the evidence for the pecking order theory is more pronounced than for the optimal capital structure theory. The optimal capital structure is not a single point, rather it is a range of values from zero to the industry mean within which a typical U.S. firm will be indifferent to the firm's debt level. Our results confirm the usefulness of taking growth of assets, fixed asset ratio, R & D expenditure, and advertising expenditure as the determinants of a firm capital structure. Our results have also shown that there is no systematic relationship between industrial concentration and debt ratios of firms belonging to that industry. Moreover, the stock prices of most companies go down significantly when a firm announces a substantial amount of new stock offerings. We have found that there is a positive and significant association between executive compensations and the debt these firms incur. We have also found that there is an inverse relationship between managerial share ownership and the percentage of debt in the firm's capital structure for NYSE firms, but not for the NASDAQ firms. Finally, NYSE firms are found to exhibit a strong inverse relationship between firm profitability and the amount of debt in the firm's capital structure. But no such relationship between profitability and capital structure is found for the AMEX firms.

Capital Structure Theory: Any Verdict Now?

Along with the optimal capital structure theory and the pecking order theory there evolved another competing theory of firm capital structure, that is, Michael Jensen's Free Cash Flow theory. Jensen and Meckling's seminal article in 1976 laid the foundation of Agency Cost theory in managerial behavior, but Jensen's 1986 article actually brought forth free cash flow as an important ingredient in modern capital structure theory. While the optimal capital structure theory emphasizes the role of corporate tax shields and financial distress, and the pecking order theory stresses on the role of asymmetric information, Jensen's cash flow theory underscores the place of agency costs in the capital structure decision-making process of the firms. Unfortunately, all three of them are conditional theories, not the complete theory we would like to have.

Optimal capital structure theory follows the neoclassical economics tradition of finding an equilibrium capital structure where the benefit of corporate tax shield is just offset by the cost of financial distress, the latter meaning bankruptcy, reorganization, and other attendant costs. This theory held sway in the capital structure discussions for a while because some of its predictions came true, as we find evident in the financial literature. For example, the theory predicts that mature firms with more tangible assets would borrow more than firms with more intangible assets, such as copyrights, goodwill, patent rights, and so on. Many empirical studies had confirmed this fact. Also, some "event" studies had showed that the announcements of the issuance of bonds drove stock prices up, while the announcements of issuing common stocks pushed stock prices down. As the firms are presumed to have target debt ratios, this proves that firms are moving toward reaching the optimum by retiring stocks to achieve that balance. The main allure of the optimal structure theory is its intuitive appeal, that is, a balancing act that keeps debt ratios from going too high.

But the optimal capital structure theory is a static trade-off theory. It got a rude awaking when more empirical results started to pour in. First, it has been found overwhelmingly that there is an inverse relationship between profitability and debt ratios of companies, which is also supported by our study. But this contradicts the main tenet of the optimal capital structure theory where high profits mean more debt to take advantage of the tax shields. It also means that firms can take more risks without exposing itself to financial distress, thus leading toward higher target-debt ratios. Second, as already mentioned, firms with higher tangible assets generally have more debts than firms with more intangible assets. The former firms are more mature firms with assets firmly in place, while the latter firms are more nascent with future earnings full of uncertainty and risks. Third, firms with higher growth opportunities tend to have lower debt ratios. These firms generally finance their projects more by dipping into retained earnings than going to the external markets for financing. Finally, the trade-off theory assumes that firms will exercise their tax shields to the limit until the financial distress costs exceed it. But many successful companies purposefully keep their debt ratios low and do not take advantage of their tax shields. As Harris and Raviv (1991) have found, the most profitable companies in an industry generally borrow the least. It is no use blaming the managers for not taking advantage of the tax shields, for they generally do not pay attention to tax savings when considering their financial designs.

There are murmurs in the finance literature about the dissatisfaction with the optimum capital structure theory. Baumol (1965) long ago had pointed out that managers would tend to avoid stock markets because of the "punishment from the impersonal mechanism of the stock exchange." So the managers would choose debt financing than equity financing. Also, Professor Donaldson (1984) in his case studies had found evidence of the pecking order, that is, firms choose internal financing first, and after exhausting that option, would choose external financing where they again choose bonds first and equity only as the last resort. But before Myers and Majluf's article in 1984, it was thought of as managerial behavior rather than efforts to maximize shareholders' wealth.

But when Myers with his co-author Majluf brought out the pecking order theory, the world was ready, as it were, to embrace it enthusiastically. Myers had pointed out that profitable firms borrow less because they can stash away more money as internal financing (in the form of retained earnings). Only the less profitable firms will resort to external financing, that is, incur debt. Also, we should remember that when it comes to external financing, firms will use debt first and then equity as the last resort. Issuing debt induces the stock price of the firm to go up, because of asymmetric information, that is, managers know more of the firm than the outside investors. So the announcement of a debt issue will increase the stock price, while issuance of common stock will lower the price of the stock because the managers think that they are overvalued. As debt is safer than equity, the asymmetric information would drive the firm to issue debt rather than equity, thus minimizing the managers' information advantage. It has been found by many empirical studies that that was the case in the real world. Apart from explaining better the negative relationship between profitability and debt ratios of firms, the pecking order theory also explains why almost all corporate equity financing has been generated by retained earnings rather than by issuing new shares.

Shyam-Sunder and Myers (1999) tested both the optimal capital structure theory and the pecking order theory, and found support for both the theories. While the pecking order theory generates mean-reverting debt ratios, the target-adjustment model of optimal capital structure "explains" this financial strategy as well. But Shyam-Sunder and Myers also proved that the testing of the pecking order theory had better statistical power relative to the optimal capital structure theory, and that the pecking order theory had the best explanation of the financial behavior of firms in their sample. Our study has also shown that both the theories co-exist, but that the pecking order theory explains the data better than the optimal capital structure theory.

In the pecking order theory, however, there is no room for managers' incentive schemes for the debt-equity choice. But as Steven Ross (1977) had pointed out in his signaling equilibrium theory, managers' compensating package can have a significant role to play regarding the issuance of bonds or common stocks. As we have found in our empirical study, executive compensation is positively correlated with debt ratios of firms. Dybvig and Zender (1991) had shown that the predictions by the pecking order theory could also be generated by alternative models in which managers' compensation incentives could play an important role in deciding the optimal capital structure.

Professors Jensen and Meckling (1976) in their path-breaking article proposed the theory of agency costs where the managers were viewed as following their self-interests that may conflict with the interests of the stockholders. To align the managers with the shareholders' value-maximizing goals, there would be "agency costs" incurred by the firms. Later on Jensen (1986) introduced the problem of "free cash flow" of the firms, which, if not checked, would lead to wasteful investments. To quote Professor Jensen in this regard, "The problem is how to motivate managers to disgorge the cash rather than investing it below the cost of capital or wasting it on organizational inefficiencies." From this viewpoint arose the organizational theory of capital structure where it is presumed that managers work for the maximization of corporate wealth over which they have effective control. If that is the case, then the managers would increase the debt level of firms to such an extent that all positive net present value projects would be financed and no excess cash would be left in the till. The history of the 1980s bore this out when leverage buyouts, restructuring, and debt-financed takeovers became quite rampant in the United States economy.

Thus the organizational theory would emphasize why debt-for-equity changes serve the best interest of the stockholders. But it also stipulates that in the majority of cases firms would not undertake this change without the threat of takeovers. The organizational theory of capital structure also explains why the most profitable firms borrow the least in the outside market. They would retain their higher profits if new investment opportunities do not come forth, rather than paying out higher dividends. Thus higher earnings would lead to higher retained earnings, and less dependence on external financing, leading to a lower debt ratio. But as Myers (2001) has pointed out, the free cash flow theory is not really a theory about the choice of managers of debt vs. equity, rather it is a theory about the consequences of high debt ratios.

We have to understand that none of these three theories offers a general theory of capital structure choice. Rather, they are conditional theories applicable to a particular set of test data, or a situation faced by a firm. The general theory has to come from the world where we also consider human capital, besides financial capital, as Hart (1995) and others have pointed out. It will be the co-integration of human and financial capital—the choice firms will face more in the future in this era of the IT (information technology) revolution.

References

Baumol, W., 1965, *The Stock Market and Economic Efficiency,* New York: Fordham University Press.

Donaldson, G., 1984, *Managing Corporate Wealth: The Operation of a Comprehensive Financial Goal System*, New York: Praeger Publishers.

Dybvig, P. H., and Jaime Zender, 1991, "Capital Structure and Dividend Irrelevance With Asymmetric Information," *Review of Financial Studies*, 4, 201-19.

Fosberg, R. and A. Ghosh (2005), "Capital Structure Changes in NYSE and NASDAQ Firms," Working Paper, William Paterson University.

Harris, M., and A. Raviv, 1991, "The Theory of Capital Structure," *Journal of Finance,* March, 46, 297-355.

Hart, O., 1995, *Firms, Contracts and Capital Structure*, Oxford: Oxford University Press.

Jensen, M.C., and William H. Meckling, 1976, "Theory of the Firm: Managerial Behavior, Agency Costs and Ownership Structure," *Journal of Financial Economics, 3, 305-360.*

Jensen, M.C., 1986, "Agency Costs of Free Cash Flow, Corporate Finance and Takeovers," *American Economic Review*, 76, 323-29.

Myers, S. C., and N. S. Majluf, 1984, "Corporate Financing and Investment Decisions When Firms Have Information That Investors Do Not Have," *Journal of Financial Economics*, 13, 187-221.

Myers, S. C., 1984, "The Capital Structure Puzzle," *Journal of Finance*, July, 39, 575-92.

_________, 2001, "Capital Structure," *Journal of Economic Perspective*, Spring, 15, 81-102.

Ross, S. A., 1977, "The Determination of Financial Structure: The Incentive-Signalling Approach," *Bell Journal of Economics*, 8, 23-40.

Shyam-Sunder, L. and S. C. Myers, 1999, "Testing Static Tradeoff Against Pecking Order Models of Capital Structure," *Journal of Financial Economics*, 51, 219-44.

Bibliography

Altman, E., 1984, "A Further Empirical Investigation of the Bankruptcy Cost Questions," *Journal of Finance* 39, 1067-1089.

Asquith, P. and D. W. Mullins, Jr., 1986, "Equity Issues and Offering Dilution," *Journal of Financial Economics* 15, 61-89.

Auerback, A., 1985, "Real Determinants of Corporate Leverage," in B. M. Friedman, ed. *Corporate Capital Structures in the United States*, Chicago: University of Chicago Press, 301-24.

Baker, M. P. and W. Jeffrey, 2001, "Market Timing and Capital Structure," Yale International Center for Finance, *Working Paper*, No. 00-32.

Barclay, M. J., C. W. Smith, Jr., and R. W. Watts, 1995, "The Determinants of Corporate Leverage and Dividend Policies," *Journal of Applied Corporate Finance* 7, 4-19.

——, 1999, "The Capital Structure Puzzle: Another Look at the Evidence," *Journal of Applied Corporate Finance* 12, 8-20.

Baskin, J., 1989, "An Empirical Examination of the Pecking Order Hypothesis," *Financial Management* 18, 26-35.

Brealey, R. A. and S. C. Myers, 2000, *Principles of Corporate Finance*, New York: McGraw-Hill.

Brav, A. and P. A. Gompers, 1997, "Myth or Reality: The Long Run Under-Performance of Initial Public Offerings: Evidence from Venture and Non-Venture Capital-Backed Companies," *Journal of Finance* 52, 1791-1822.

Castenias, R., 1983, "Bankruptcy Risk and Optimal Capital Structure," *Journal of Finance* 38, 1617-1635.

DeAngelo, H. and R. W. Masulis, 1980, "Optimal Capital Structure under Corporate and Personal Taxation," *Journal of Financial Economics* 8, 3-30.

Donaldson, G., 1984, *Managing Corporate Wealth: The Operation of a Comprehensive Financial Goal System*, New York: Praeger.

Durant, D., 1959, "The Cost of Debt and Equity Funds for Businesses," in E. Solomon, Ed., *The Management of Corporate Capital*, New York: Free Press.

——, 1959, "The Cost of Capital, Corporation Finance and the Theory of Investment: Comment," *American Economic Review* 49, 639-655.

Dybvig, P. and J. F. Zender, 1991, "Capital Structure and Dividend Irrelevance with Asymmetric Information," *Review of Financial Studies* 4, 201-19.

Fama, E., 1978, "The Effects of a Firm's Financing and Investment Decisions on the Welfare of its Security Holders," *American Economic Review* 68, 274-284.

Fama, E. and K. R. French, 1998, "Taxes, Financing Decisions, and Firm Value," *Journal of Finance* 53, 819-43.

——, 2003, "Financing Decision: Who Issue Stocks?" CRSP *Working Paper*, No. 549.

Gilson, S. C., K. John, and L. H. P. Lang, "Troubled Debt Restructurings: An Empirical Study of Private Reorganization of Firms in Default," *Journal of Financial Economics* 27, 315-353.

Harris, M. and A. Raviv, 1991, "The Theory of Capital Structure," *Journal of Finance* 46, 297-355.

Jalilvand, A. and R. S. Harris, "Corporate Behavior in Adjusting to Capital Structure and Dividend Targets: An Econometric Study," *Journal of Finance* 39, 127-144.

Jensen, M. C. and W. H. Mackling, 1976, "Theory of the Firm: Managerial Behavior, Agency Costs, and Ownership Structure," *Journal of Financial Economics* 3, 305-360.

Loughran, T. and J. R. Ritter, 1997, "Ownership Structure: Conducting Seasoned Equity Offerings," *Journal of Finance* 52, 1823-1850.

Leland, H. and D. Pyle, 1977, "Information Asymmetries, Financial Structure, and Financial Intermediation," *Journal of Finance* 32, 371-387.

Magginson, W. L., 1997, *Corporate Finance Theory*, Springfield, MA: Addison-Wesley, Chapter 7.

Mickelson, W. and M. M. Partch, 1986, "Valuation Effects of Security Offerings and the Issuance Process," *Journal of Financial Economics* 15, 31-60.

Miller, M., 1977, "Death and Taxes," *Journal of Finance* 32, 261-276.

——, 1989, "The Modigliani-Miller Propositions After Thirty Years," *Journal of Applied Corporate Finance* 2, 6-18.

Modigliani, F. and M. Miller, 1958, "The Cost of Capital, Corporate Finance, and the Theory of Investments," *American Economic Review* 48, 261-297.

——, 1963, "Corporate Income Taxes and the Cost of Capital: A Correction," *American Economic Review* 53, 433-443.

Myers, S. C., 1984, "The Capital Structure Puzzle," *Journal of Finance*, 575-592.

——, 1993, "Still Searching for Optimal Capital Structure," *Journal of Applied Corporate Finance* 1, 4-14.

——, 2001, "Capital Structure," *Journal of Economic Perspectives* 15, 81-102.

——and N. S. Majluf, 1984, "Corporate Financing and Investment Decisions When Firms have Information Investors do not Have," *Journal of Financial Economics* 43, 187-221.

Rajan, R. G. and L. Zingales, 1995, "What Do We Know about Capital Structure? Some Evidence from International Data," *Journal of Finance* 50, 1421-1460.

Ross, S. A., 1977, "The Determination of Financial Structure: The Incentive-Signaling Approach, *Bell Journal of Economics* 8, 23-40.

Shyam-Sunder, L. and S. C. Myers, "Testing Static Trade Off Against Pecking Order Model of Capital Structure," *Journal of Financial Economics* 51, 219-44.

Solomon, E., ed., 1959, *The Management of Corporate Capital*, New York: Free Press.

Stiglitz, J. E., 1969, "A Reexamination of the Modigliani-Miller Theorem," *American Economic Review* 54, 784-793.

Taggart, Jr., R. A., 1985, "Secular Patterns in the Financing of U.S. Corporations," in B. M. Friedman (ed.), *Corporate Capital Structures in the United States,* Chicago: University of Chicago Press.

Wald, J. K., 1999, "How Firm Characteristics Affect Capital Structure," *Journal of Financial Research* 22, 161-87.

Zingales, L, 2000, "In Search of New Foundations," *Journal of Finance* 55, 1623-53

Index

CPSIA information can be obtained at www.ICGtesting.com
Printed in the USA
BVOW012212020412

286685BV00002B/5/P

9 781412 847551